Lives of the Musicians

Amy Winehouse

Kate Solomon

Laurence King Publishing

LAURENCE KING

Published in 2021 by
Laurence King Publishing Ltd
361–373 City Road
London EC1V 1LR
United Kingdom
T + 44 (0)20 7841 6900
enquiries@laurenceking.com
www.laurenceking.com

A catalogue record for this book is available
from the British Library.

ISBN: 978-1-78627-884-5

Printed in Italy

Laurence King Publishing is committed to ethical
and sustainable production. We are proud participants
in The Book Chain Project®
bookchainproject.com

Cover illustration: Rik Lee

CONTENTS

Introduction

In very basic psychology lessons, you learn about some-thing called 'flashbulb memories'. These are the vivid memories that are seared instantly into your brain when something particularly shocking or emotional happens. When someone asks where you were on 9/11 and you can almost smell the cut grass of the lawn you were walking by, that's a flashbulb memory. For some of us – music fans, Amy fans, gossip hounds, journalists – 23 July 2011 is one of those. I remember it very clearly – I was walking out of Holland Park with my then boyfriend. It was a sunny day, and I was checking my phone when a tweet caught my eye: '10 celebrities who died too young'. I clicked through and among the Kurt Cobains and James Deans, there was Amy Winehouse. I laughed, saying to my boyfriend, 'Someone's getting fired – they've included Amy Winehouse in this. She's still alive!'

It was a time when obituaries were occasionally and accidentally posted before their time, and we were all morbidly aware of (and fascinated by) the fact that newspapers had pre-written remembrances for celebrities who might not have been long for this world. I have no doubt that every newspaper and celebrity-adjacent media outlet had something prepared for Amy Winehouse. She spent so much of her time tiptoeing the line between life and death, and we were so aware of it, thanks to the story-hungry media that egged her on. For weeks at a time, tabloids featured that towering beehive in various states of disarray on the front pages every day. Even if you didn't read tabloids, you experienced the Amy Winehouse Downfall in real time, to the point where it began to feel like we were all simply waiting for the worst to happen.

On that July day, after five years of half-expecting it, Amy's death was still a horrible shock. Hence my willingness to believe the listicle I'd clicked on was published in human error. We'd watched her reach rock bottom, but we also thought we'd seen her claw her way back up. That story arc was over, now comes the redemption; the next album; the wedding; the kids; the mundanity of sobriety, of middle age. Amy managed to make music that was almost universally enjoyed, but people who identified as her fans tended to be young women, around Amy's age or slightly younger, who felt more of an affinity with her and her rough edges than they did with the Katy Perrys and the Miley Cyruses of the world – even the wronged good girl Adele was more your mum's speed than your own. But Amy felt real. The relationship fans had with her felt like a personal one, her narrative-heavy songs like long texts sent late at night. Amy would say exactly what she thought. She'd go to the pub and drink you under the table, she'd cheat and lie and make mistakes, but she was *human*, with all the pain and mess that comes with it. She was so alive that even when she was on the cusp of death, it didn't feel like something that could happen.

Who is culpable in the tragedy of Amy Winehouse? Many seek to attribute blame to any one of a cast of characters that Shakespeare himself could have dreamt up: the untrustworthy ex-husband who used her devotion to him to fund his drug habit and, in turn, caused hers; the withholding, fame-hungry father; the mother who had to put her own health ahead of her daughter's; the record label that saw Amy Winehouse as a cash cow; the devoted friends who simply reached the end of their rope with her; and the media, a heaving, seething mess of flashbulbs and column inches, which used Amy as a one-woman soap opera to sell papers and ad space. And what of Amy's responsibility for herself? A woman who was seen as a fearless, say-anything figure but pleaded for strength to come from elsewhere ('Stronger Than Me'); a woman who told us repeatedly how much she was struggling but couldn't accept help from anyone but herself.

But of course, hindsight is 20/20 and addiction is a bitch. There may be villains in the Amy Winehouse story, but we could any one of us point to ourselves, even, for our role in events. We lapped up songs that were so obviously ripped from a broken heart, and laughed when Amy became the butt of jokes. When she stumbled on stage high, or appeared on television completely out of it, we tutted and said to ourselves, 'She's not going to last long if she carries on this way.' I like to think that now, we might be more empathetic towards anyone in that state, but more recent events like the tragedy of Caroline Flack suggest that we still enjoy vilifying certain public figures to the point that they be hounded to death. Amy's lifelong mental health issues, eating disorders and addictions were harder to bear than I think any of us realized, masked as they were by that ear-to-ear grin and her immensely affecting voice.

The stories of Amy's life threatened to overwhelm the music she made – but in fact, her music and her story are one and the same. Amy couldn't write songs unless she felt them deep in her heart. If *Frank* is a snapshot of a girl proving she's a woman, *Back to Black* is the portrait in oils that haunted her for the rest of her life. It's a shame that she didn't have the chance to dig deeper; to really exorcize the sadness inside her that she kept hidden from everyone, even herself. A sadness, too, that she never trusted that she could find help outside her own head. A lifelong distrust of therapists, doctors and sustained care was the biggest stumbling block in what could – should – have been the story of her recovery. Perhaps, if we'd been lucky, she would have examined her illnesses in later life and made something beautiful from them, just as she did with the heartbreak that almost killed her in 2006.

No one comes out of Amy's story looking good, least of all Amy herself. It's not my intention to romanticize someone who could just as easily be a violent bully as she could be your most caring friend. Boredom often made her acidic, but it also kept her sharp. From the poems scribbled in her school books while she was meant to be paying attention, to the songs she won Grammys and Ivor Novellos for, she twisted language and broke conventions to create something that felt like it was written just for you. If she were here, my guess is that she'd be as unapologetic about the chaos of her life and death as she was when she was alive. She'd shrug and say, 'That's how it is', then throw a punchline over her shoulder that would have you laughing till bedtime.

How cruel it was to lose Amy at 27. But how lucky we are to have what she left behind.

1

'Oh Shit!'

Amy Jade Winehouse was born at the end of a mild, dry summer. In what would soon be known as typical Amy fashion, she arrived four days late, making her entrance at night as rain pounded down on Enfield, north London. Her mother, Janis, had spent the entire pregnancy convinced that she was having another boy. Four years earlier she'd given birth to Alex, and although she couldn't explain what hormonal alchemy had made her believe he was going to have a little brother, she felt it so strongly that the idea of having a girl simply did not register. When the midwife finally held Amy up and announced, 'It's a girl!', a delirious and exhausted Janis was so surprised that she shouted out, 'Oh shit!' From her very first moments on earth, Amy was bucking expectations.

Among the things that needed to be rethought was the baby's name. Taking the first letter of a deceased loved one's name for a child's is a Jewish tradition, and Janis and her husband, Mitchell (Mitch), had decided to name the son they thought was coming for Janis's grandmother, Annie. It didn't take much to switch the name they'd settled on, Ames, to Amy; they also added Jade, named for Mitch's stepfather, Jack. Amy Jade Winehouse was officially out in the world.

It might not have seemed like it at the time, but 1983 was a pivotal year. It was the year that the internet was officially born, the year that the first mobile cellular call was made and the first games console, the Nintendo Famicom, went on sale. These leaps in technology meant that life was about to lurch in a strange new direction, although we didn't know it yet. We might think nothing of filming every moment of a young child's life now, but in the 1980s only the reasonably wealthy had the means to invest hundreds of pounds in a camcorder. It was typical Mitch that, although he had recently lost his job as a salesman, he returned home one day with a chunky JVC camera to document Amy and Alex's early childhood. He describes himself as 'besotted' with his baby daughter, filming every moment he could and panicking at every strange sound that came from her cot, although most of the parenting responsibility – dirty nappies, sleepless nights – was left to his wife. But actually, Amy ended up being quite an easy baby. Sometimes Janis even had to gently wake her up for midnight feeds. Alex had been desperate for a younger brother, but he soon got used to the responsibilities of having a sister. As Amy got older, they became inseparable and his parents often found him sitting by Amy's cot, as if guarding her from harm.

The day after Amy's birth, Mitch finally admitted to Janis that he'd lost his job. He dressed as sharply as ever when he came to visit her on the maternity ward, sat down heavily and put his head in his hands: 'Janis, there's something I've got to tell you.' Mitch had always had a bit of a wheeler-dealer streak; it had stood him in good stead in the early eighties, when money tended to reward ambition, so Janis wasn't too worried about him finding more work. His tendency to act on instinct made him an exciting husband, and he always seemed to land on his feet. Still, the timing wasn't great: not only did they have a newborn and a toddler to look after, they'd recently moved from a small flat to a larger suburban home with a bigger mortgage.

The new house was on a leafy street in Southgate, north London. It was much more spacious than their old flat and meant that baby Amy got her own nursery, decorated in cheerful yellow wallpaper with marshmallow clouds. There's a running joke in Janis's family that all the women have exactly the same features, and Amy was no exception: a mop of curly dark hair framed her face, often pulled down into a determined frown as she figured things out, but just as often opening into the broad grin she shared with her mother and grandmother. She grew into a bright, inquisitive girl with a loud cry and an unshakable devotion to her big brother. 'Alex' was her first proper word and just another sign that Amy was desperate to copy everything that he did; whether it was practising his Bar Mitzvah speech or colouring in or singing, Amy wanted to do the same – only Amy wanted to do it bigger and louder.

She took her first shaky steps on her first birthday and from then on it was impossible to keep her in one place; she was soon known in the extended family as Hurricane Amy. With hair sticking out in every direction, she'd barrel into a room and fill every nook with incessant chatter and a seemingly endless source of energy. Her inquisitive palate also got her into trouble – the first time Amy had her stomach pumped it was because she'd eaten a toadstool from a neighbour's garden. There wasn't a climbing frame she wouldn't leap from, or a playground she wouldn't tear off into, constantly giving her parents scares as she flung herself over bars in the park. She loved to dance and put on shows with Alex for their parents' enjoyment. Her brother would soon get bored and wander off, but Amy would keep singing, louder and louder, and 'Be quiet, Amy!' became a common refrain around the house. Janis sums her young daughter up best: 'full of energy and impossible to ignore.'

In fact, even as a child, Amy was terrified of being ignored. Her family talk about how clingy she could be – particularly Janis, who happened to be working at Amy's nursery school. She'd be trying to work with other children and Amy would barge her way in and monopolize her. She hated to share her, much more insecure than her outgoing personality first suggested. Her attention-seeking didn't always rely on a tug of the maternal arm or a song relayed at the top of her voice, either. It hit new heights one day when she was about seven years old, playing in the grassy expanse of Broomfield Park. Janis was chatting to a friend while Amy went about, crouching down by the waterside to bother the ducks, grubbing about for worms, running from swings to roundabouts and back again. Chat over, Janis called for her but was met only with silence and a growing sense of panic. She must be here somewhere, Janis thought. Amy was known for constantly wriggling free and running off, but she wouldn't leave the park, would she? Frantically asking everyone she passed if they'd seen a little girl with dark hair and dark eyes, Janis felt more and more sick with every minute that she couldn't find her daughter. As dusk fell and the family-wide search failed, hopes dwindled. The police told Janis there wasn't much more she could do that evening and that she should go home. But just as she was considering leaving, someone spotted a mop of curly hair by the park gates. It was Amy, grinning wildly, hand in hand with Mitch's sister Melody.

Any parent will know the overwhelming sense of relief at locating a missing child, whether they've been gone for five minutes or five hours. They'll also know the flush of anger that accompanies it – what was she *thinking*? A friend of Melody's had come across Amy apparently alone in the park and invited her back to play at her house. Bored of waiting for her mum, Amy had enthusiastically agreed and, although the friend had called Melody to let her know where Amy was, the message hadn't made its way back to the frantic family. Amy, naturally, was thrilled with the situation. It helped give rise to her other family nickname – 'Nudge', a Yiddish word for a pest but used by the family to mean that she was always pushing her luck – and the story became Winehouse family lore.

One of the few people who commanded respect from Amy was her grandmother, Cynthia Winehouse. She was a tough old broad who'd lived about a thousand lives. In the sixties she had been in a singing group with her sister and had dated Ronnie Scott, the jazz musician whose name has become synonymous with one of the best jazz clubs in London. As well as helping to inspire Amy's love of jazz, one sharp word from Cynthia could knock Amy back into line. The two became very close as Amy grew up; visiting her grandmother was one of the few appointments that

Amy always arrived at on time and looking presentable. Cynthia saw things in Amy that it took others longer to catch on to: she encouraged her to attend performing arts school and ferried her to and from auditions. There was a vogue for holding seances in the eighties, and Cynthia was a big proponent of them. She'd invite friends and family round every Tuesday and commune with the spirits: when Amy was about five years old, Cynthia received a message about her. 'Someone always needs to look out for Amy', the voice said. Later, Cynthia would be the first person to realize that Amy was an alcoholic.

Headstrong determination coupled with childish insecurity were personality traits that would follow Amy into adulthood. In almost every interview there's a moment where her attention wanders and her answers become monosyllabic and bored, or she'll sulk and refuse to talk, or she'll be so charming and giggly it's like chatting to that mischievous seven-year-old who disappeared without thinking of the consequences. She could wrap people round her little finger if she wanted to, even as a young child – and she could throw tantrums like nobody's business. In a video shot at her fourth birthday party, dressed in an extremely eighties outfit of lime green T-shirt and cycle shorts, she wanders around apart from her friends. One minute she's monkeying around with Mitch, the next twisting away from his grasp and falling to the ground, beating the floor with her hands. But after a dressing-down from her mother, she folds her arms defiantly and looks across the gymnasium directly into the camera, then scampers out of view into a hallway.

Mitch and Janis had a reasonably happy marriage during Amy's early life – or, as happy as it can be when one half of the partnership is naturally itchy-footed and constantly on the road. As the children got older, the relationship became less and less stable. At the same time, Mitch's business was in gradual decline. Janis felt that she'd been left to raise the children alone, while Mitch's increasingly mysterious behaviour included weekend trips to Bolton that were so frequent that 'Bolton' became shorthand for an unexplained disappearance among Janis's friends. Mitch's returns to the family home were always met with excitement from his daughter, who doted on him (his tendency to come laden with gifts probably didn't hurt). She thought of him as two different people – Daddy Mitchell was the dad who was there when she got home from school but wished he was elsewhere, and Mitch Winehouse was the man who'd spend hours telling her family legends and tales of his adventures. Eventually, it became clear to Janis that he'd met another woman and was having an affair.

When Amy was around nine years old her parents split, and Mitch left the family home to live with his new partner, Jane. Amy seemed to take the whole thing in her stride; she burst into giggles on the day that they sombrely sat her and Alex down to tell them the news, and on the day that Mitch moved out, Amy turned to Janis and said, 'Dad's gone. Can we get a hamster?' Weeks, maybe months before, Janis had become so sick of Amy's constant pestering for a new pet, she had exasperatedly told her she could have one when her dad had moved out. Janis forgot; Amy certainly didn't. (She got the hamster, named Penfold for Danger Mouse's bespectacled sidekick.) But Amy's desire for attention from withholding men could well have stemmed from the loss of her father from the family home; it probably fed into her tendency to use baby voices and wheedle favours and attention out of them. It almost certainly didn't help her burgeoning insecurities.

Before Amy had been born, Janis had started to feel a tingling sensation in her hands and feet. After several trips to the doctors, she was told that it could be multiple sclerosis, a terrifying prospect for anyone, but especially a young mother with two small children to care for. MS can cause loss of sensation in the limbs and lead to impaired mobility and vision, alongside other debilitating symptoms. But after Amy's birth, the tingling seemed to subside and Janis put it to the back of her mind; there were other things to focus on than her health.

Of all the significant relationships Amy formed as a child, perhaps the most important was with Juliette Ashby. The two met at Osidge Primary School, where they became fierce friends and would remain so pretty much constantly for the rest of Amy's life. In class, you'd find them giggling at the back, and in the playground they practised dance routines for their Salt-N-Pepa tribute act (named, adorably, Sweet'N'Sour), or pretended to be Wham!'s backing singers (Juliette was always Pepsi, Amy was Shirley). They were friends in the way that only young girls can be – inseparable, honest with each other and constantly, constantly in trouble. When they returned to Osidge Primary School for a newspaper feature about friendship in 2007, they disappeared off into the school hall and, minutes later, the fire alarm went off. 'Thing is', Amy said at the time, 'we always wanted to do that when we were here.' 'But we never had the bottle', Juliette agreed. It seemed almost inevitable that they'd return to complete the work that their younger selves had begun. When they graduated to secondary school, both girls' parents tried to bolster their grades by requesting they be placed in different classes – which worked. They drifted apart, driven in different directions by their adolescent attempts to discover who they were – but at 16, Amy and Juliette were back together.

It might not surprise anyone to learn that academic study wasn't high up Amy's list of priorities. She was wickedly clever but completely bored by school, which didn't help much with her tendency to trouble-make. She was always playing ringleader at school, which meant the other kids were faced with one of two Amys: the fiercely loyal and super-protective mama bear, or the spiteful, aggressive bully. On a good day, Amy was charming, funny and kind – but on a bad day she was loud and disruptive, and often hard to be around unless you were in her inner circle. 'Complicated' and 'troublesome' are two words that her mother used to describe Amy as a child – they could just as easily be attributed to the woman she grew into.

Amy began to really struggle during her teens. She developed a habit of over-sleeping – often a sign of depression – and talked in later years about turning to self-harm to try to control her emotions. Reading about her now, it sounds exhausting to have maintained these disparate personalities – the attention-seeking drama queen, the caring daughter and friend, the frustration of being forced to focus on other things when all she wanted to do was sing. She wrote poetry during this period – short, biographical vignettes with the timbre and humour of her songs – and they have an air of freedom about them, even the nonsense poems written in her rough book at the back of science class. 'I really just want to sing, Mum', she'd pout. What she was doing, obviously, was writing songs; and it seemed as though writing them was the only time she really relaxed into herself.

Her love of music was a constant throughout her life. It had begun in the womb, with Janis playing classical music to the bump, then developed through the radio stations her brother listened to, and eventually matured into a deep, long-held love of jazz, thanks to Mitch and Cynthia. When she liked something, she *really* liked it, listening to the same songs over and over and over again. 'My brother was listening to stuff like Sonic Youth and Pearl Jam and Therapy, really, like, I-want-to-die bands. I had a really brief flirtation with that, but I must have been nine – and then I discovered Salt-N-Pepa and I was like: I've got my music now', she said later. Then, Alex discovered Thelonious Monk. Amy was about 14 at the time. 'I just remember the first time I ever heard [Monk's] ''Round Midnight', through the wall. I was just like: what is that? And I remember the first time I heard Ray Charles. It was 'Unchain My Heart'. I remember walking into my brother's room … and he goes, "What?" He looked at me as if I was about to go, "Mum's dead" or something (touch wood). He goes, "What's wrong?", and I went: "Who is this?" And he went: "It's Ray Charles." Then I just listened to Ray Charles for three months, exclusively.'

At an end-of-term concert at her secondary school, Amy blew everyone away with her rendition of Alanis Morissette's hit 'Ironic'. Although she'd been in school plays (memorably as Rizzo in *Grease*) and even on a West End stage in an English National Opera production of *Don Quixote*, the Alanis cover was the first time her parents realized she could really *sing*. As they congratulated her afterwards, she shrugged and said, 'Yeah, it was ok.'

When they realized what a natural she was on stage, Janis and Mitch were much more open to the idea of sending Amy to stage school. At 13, she applied for a scholarship to the Sylvia Young Theatre School, a performing arts school in central London that is still seen as a stepping-stone to superstardom, thanks to a roster of famous alumni including Dua Lipa, members of Little Mix and All Saints. The Winehouses weren't wealthy by any stretch, but with the scholarship and Mitch's uncanny ability to generate money when it was needed, they could just about manage the fees. Sylvia Young herself recalls Amy's ambitious application form, which even at 13 contained many elements of the things Amy would continue to cite in her press interviews even at the height of her success: a desire to take people away from their troubles, to be allowed to sing all the time, to stretch herself – and even some of her trademark humour. 'I want to go somewhere where I am stretched right to my limits and perhaps even beyond', she wrote. 'To sing in lessons without being told to shut up (provided they are singing lessons). But mostly, I have this dream to be very famous. To work on stage. It's a lifelong ambition. I want people to hear my voice and just … forget their troubles for five minutes. I want to be remembered for being an actress, a singer for sell-out concerts and sell-out West End and Broadway shows. For being … just me.'

It's tempting to say that Amy as a child was Amy the woman in microcosm, already bristling with all the elements for which she'd be known as an adult: temperamentality, charm, talent and headstrong self-belief, tempered by insecurity in her relationships and a fear of being alone. But although her parents may reckon they always knew there was something special about Amy, when you watch back all the video footage her family and friends shot, and consider the accounts of her childhood exploits, she was just a girl like any other, trying to find safe footing in a world that already felt unsteady under her feet.

2

'Honestly, I'm Not Wasting Time'

In 1996, pop music was dominated by the opposing poles of the Spice Girls, with their flashy quasi-feminism and bash-you-round-the-head pop songs, and the Fugees' gently heartbreaking jazz-tinged cover of 'Killing Me Softly'. Strange futuristic leaps occurred that made us question the very nature of life when Dolly the sheep was born, and cultural shockwaves were felt when Charles and Diana divorced. But presumably unperturbed by all this was 13-year-old Amy Winehouse, excited to leave Ashmole School and start at Sylvia Young. 'Her abilities could put her in the same league as Judy Garland or Ella Fitzgerald', Sylvia wrote in 2007. 'She could be one of the greats.'

Amy loved it. A world away from the laced-up world of endless book learning, she got to spend hours each day performing, learning how to use her voice and her body to express herself in classes like ballet, tap, acting and singing. She was soon bumped up a year, partly because of her talent, but partly in an effort to keep her engaged and prevent her disruptive tendencies coming out. She also made a formative friend during her first weeks at the school: Tyler James, a sweet, pointy-faced boy with a passion for music.

At home it became 'Tyler this, Tyler that' as she babbled about her new friend, glowing with the excitement of meeting a kindred spirit – someone who understood how she used music to make sense of her world. It was also while she was commuting across London to Sylvia Young's that she discovered Camden, the London borough she'd become synonymous with and where she spent more and more time hanging around the weirdos and misfits that peopled the bustling alternative markets and dive bars (both when she was and wasn't supposed to be at school).

Although she was now happy and fulfilled by the performance element of her schooling, Amy was still less than enthusiastic about the academic parts. Hair amok, uniform all over the place, forbidden hoop earrings in and no doubt more make-up than was generally allowed, she became just as distracting as she had been at Ashmole. One day during class, she sat at the back ignoring the teacher, and diligently and determinedly pierced, well, something. Some reports say it was her nose; her mum recalls it as her lip. Either way, not something you really want to turn around and see someone doing in the middle of a maths class. Whenever she was caught misbehaving, she'd shrug it off or feign sorrow, as she always had, and return to her antics as soon as the teacher turned away.

When Amy was 14, Janis was called in to the school for an urgent meeting about her daughter's GCSE prospects. It wasn't a long discussion: Amy was on track to fail the exams that signify the end of mandatory schooling in the UK, and the teacher in question not-so-subtly implied Janis should think about moving her to another school. Panic set in. Boredom and disinterest were not things Amy handled well, but clearly she was bright, funny, clever and creative. There was no reason she should fail her GCSEs if she would just concentrate – but she simply would not engage with the compulsory subjects that were required study, alongside the lessons that she loved. The last thing anyone wanted was for Amy to drop out of school altogether. This teacher at Sylvia Young's had been blunt and, although Janis suspected he was motivated more by self-interest than concern for Amy, she spent the next few months searching for a school that could handle her daughter. It seemed that perhaps this teacher had gone rogue when Sylvia Young herself called Janis to ask her to let Amy stay, but by then, determination to get Amy through her exams had overtaken any other emotion. She and Mitch eventually found an independent private school nearby, and that was the end of Amy's time at Sylvia Young's.

Even when they no longer saw each other every day at school, Amy and Tyler stayed firm friends. Amy also fell back in with her former best friend Juliette, spending countless hours smoking weed and being silly together in a whole new way. Amy's weed-smoking was verging on habitual in her late teens, and she often spoke of how much she liked just kicking back with a spliff and listening to music. One day she asked Janis for a lift. They piled into the car and Amy directed her to a street Janis wasn't familiar with. 'I'll just be a minute, Mum', she said, and hopped out of the passenger side, disappearing into a house for five minutes, ten, fifteen … eventually she returned and it became pretty clear to Janis that Amy had just picked up from her dealer. The sheer balls of asking your mum for a lift to pick up drugs is almost admirable; Amy was either completely oblivious or graduating to a whole new level of button-pushing.

By this point, she'd also discovered alcohol. Teenagers have ways of acquiring cheap beer, and Amy's crew was no exception. At first there would be gatherings at friends' houses, where they'd get buzzed on cans of lager, but the Winehouse family started to feel uneasy about Amy's use of alcohol at a family party. Her beloved Cynthia had asked her to sing at her husband's fiftieth birthday party; Amy was 15 and was allowed one drink, since they were all together at a private function in a north London club. Whether it was nerves for her performance, or general youthful boundary-pushing, Amy never let that glass sit empty. Alex had a word, telling her to cool it. Janis tried to tell her that enough was enough, too, but Amy made her classic move of agreeing and then carrying on anyway. Either wildly over-reacting or betraying incredible perception, Cynthia turned to Janis and said under her breath, 'She's an alcoholic.'

The new school was a strict, academic-focused all-girls school called The Mount, where Amy started in the autumn of 1998 and bucked against authority more than ever. She even seemed to lose interest in music, rankling when teachers tried to tell her how to sing in music lessons, storming out of productions and refusing to take part. She started skipping school and parent–teacher evenings became more and more fraught for Janis. Before one particularly catastrophic evening, Amy and her friends wrote notes to Janis to soften the blow of what was to come. Amy's wasn't exactly contrite, but it was another example of her playing the sweet, dutiful daughter in the face of all evidence to the contrary. While no doubt avoiding some kind of academic work, she wrote: 'To Mum, I love you so much. I don't have any work to do so, honestly, I'm not wasting time. You're a good mum. Amy.'

No one really expected Amy to continue with school after her exams. Confirming the theory that GCSEs mean next to nothing, Amy scraped a D in music, a B in English and a handful of Cs, then applied to the BRIT School in London's Croydon on a whim. She didn't last long – after a two-hour commute, her interest in the musical theatre classes she had enrolled in quickly waned, and she left one term in, leaving classmates Adele and Jessie J to continue without her. Amy seemed anchorless at this point, sometimes working in a tattoo parlour and market stall in Camden, half-heartedly joining the National Youth Jazz Orchestra as a singer and chain-smoking her way through rehearsals, and doing some local pub gigs with Juliette. All the time, she'd be scribbling notes and ideas down in the privacy of her cosy, aquatic bedroom. In a classic angsty teen move, Amy had painted her last room black (although she'd lost interest halfway through), but when Janis moved the family into a large house in Woodside Park, north London, with her then partner, Tony, Amy spent hours painting a huge Hokusai wave mural on the walls of her new room. It was cosy, always a mess and somewhere that even Janis would gravitate to for a chat when her friends visited.

Juliette's dad happened to be a big cheese at a news agency named World Entertainment News Network (WENN).

During this rudderless time, Amy started her first and only office job, writing showbiz news that would go out on the wires to newspapers and magazines around the country. She had a gift for words so it wasn't a surprise that 'journalist' was on her fairly short list of ambitions – for anyone else this would have been an incredible opportunity, and an amazing foot in the door of a notoriously competitive industry. But Amy was, once again, bored, stifled by the routine of a desk job. And, once again, it also turned out to be somewhere that put her in contact with people who'd play a formative role in her music career: it was at WENN that she met her first serious boyfriend, Chris Taylor.

Chris was sweet and sensitive, and Amy pursued him aggressively. He had deep-set puppy-dog eyes and rugged stubble. They dated for seven months before she got bored of him. It was an impossible situation: she wanted attention but she also responded to indifference; she wanted someone to take charge of her, pull her into line – perhaps even to fulfil that patriarchal role that she'd lacked in all the years that Mitch had essentially become a part-time dad – but it had to be the right kind of control, it couldn't rub her up the wrong way or lead to disinterest. They broke up at Amy's house one day and, a couple of hours later, an unsentimental Amy called to Janis, 'Mum, will you drive me to Chris's?' She was holding a cardboard box stacked with bits and pieces he'd left in her room over the past few months – T-shirts, CDs, cans of deodorant, sentimental knick-knacks, the detritus of a shared adolescent love. They drove over and within five minutes the box was handed over and it was done. 'Ok, we can go now', she announced, getting back into the car, the relationship already receding in her mind. It was one of the least messy break-ups Amy would ever go through. Although Chris wasn't the love of her life, he did play a very important and inspirational role in the months after their relationship dwindled; he's never spoken about his relationship with Amy publicly – the same couldn't exactly be said of Amy.

While Amy was dragging herself into the WENN offices every day, Tyler James had signed to Brilliant! management (soon to be renamed Brilliant 19). 'You should hear my friend Amy', he'd tell a hungry young manager named Nick Shymansky. 'She's an amazing jazz singer.' Nick was just out of school, brand new to the business and eager to prove himself. 'Looking back on it, I was 19, working in the music industry but I didn't really know anything', he recalled in 2015. 'I called her and pretended I was this big manager who could make things happen, giving it all the showbiz talk, and obviously she thought I was a wanker.' Taking it in her stride and refusing to be even slightly impressed by him, Amy played it cool with Nick – almost too cool. He came away with the impression that she had absolutely zero interest in a career as a musician. But a few days later, a jiffy bag landed in Nick's in-tray, plastered in hearts and kisses, and with 'Amy' written all over it 'about 100 times'. Classic Amy – desperate for attention but horrified at the idea of you knowing it. 'I put it on in my car', Nick said of the two-song demo. 'It blew my mind.' At just 17, Amy had the voice of an old soul, doused in emotion and sounding completely out of step with time. It was 2001, but she sounded like she'd beamed her voice directly from the 1950s. Managing to track her down for a meeting became a game of cat and mouse, but eventually Nick persuaded Amy to come to Turnham Green, near the Brilliant offices – amazingly, she actually showed up. Although she seemed nervous, they clicked instantly. Nick was able to laugh off Amy's poison-dart flirtations that tended to build their subject up before whipping the carpet out from under them with an insult that tugged at their deepest insecurities.

After seeing her sing at the jazz orchestra rehearsals, he passed her tape on to his boss, Nick Godwyn. Once again, Amy was very laissez-faire about the opportunity in front of her. She turned up for her first professional meeting and refused to play because she'd broken a guitar string, telling them she wasn't sure what she wanted to do with her life: 'I don't know really. Sing a bit – be a roller-skating waitress?' In June 2001, with the signatures of both her parents, Amy signed a four-year management deal with Brilliant 19, and received her first advance of £6,000. She quit WENN and became a full-time songwriter. Or, at least, that was the idea – in reality, Amy rarely made it to the studio on time, and would rarely focus when she did. It got to the point where the two Nicks would have to call in the big guns: Cynthia. It's fun to imagine these two music industry hot-shots having to ask their artist's granny to kick her into gear – but it worked, for a while. Eventually they decided that the easiest thing to do would be to bring the studio to Amy: thousands of pounds worth of equipment was duly installed in the corner of her bedroom, where she'd sit for hours with Juliette, producing very little in the way of work.

Luckily, it didn't take much to get producers interested in working with Amy. About five seconds listening to her voice was usually enough, and the songs she had written were also garnering interest from music publishers. Although she didn't have a record deal, Nick Shymansky negotiated a publishing deal for her with EMI in early 2002, which resulted in a £73,437 cheque. That's a lot of studded belts down at Camden Market. The whole Winehouse family was agog at this amount of money and, naturally, Amy was delighted – it meant that she could move out of her family home and into a flat in Camden with Juliette. Mitch, who coincidentally was around a lot more as Amy's career began to take off, helped her find the flat. Functional rather than opulent, Amy and Juliette's flat became a hub for their friends to gather in, surrounded by ashtrays, Amy's various cats, and the bright lights and grimy glamour of Camden.

In 2002, Camden was buzzing – there was an air of lawlessness and limitless possibility. It was the era of The Libertines and the rise of indie music, a growing subculture that seemed to favour rock'n'roll mainly as an excuse for drink and drugs. The crunching guitars and sweaty energy of this new breed of indie operated first in dive bars and later in the charts. Although Amy's music wasn't exactly indie – her early songs were jazz-focused with a kind of folkish storytelling bent – she was constantly out in Camden Town and became part of the scene. When they weren't holed up in the flat with an ounce of weed and a bunch of friends round, she and Juliette would go to gigs, drink and generally get up to no good. Amy would talk to anyone she liked the look of, and get lairy with anyone annoying her.

Nick Shymansky got Amy working with a number of producers to help hone her sound, and the demos they worked up together led to Island Records' interest in her. She strode into the record company's offices, sat down, tied her hair up and played a song, just her and her guitar in front of a room full of suits. Now that she had an actual record deal, Amy was forced to work in a slightly more structured way – but not much more. She ended up in Miami working with Salaam Remi, an amazing producer who'd worked with hip-hop legends like the Fugees and Nas. This was perfect for Amy, who wanted to blend her improvisational jazz style with vintage RnB beats to create something that sounded classic but new all at once.

The result was *Frank*. Many of the songs on this debut album were about Amy's relationship with Chris Taylor, not many of which painted him (or her) in a particularly glowing light. On 'Stronger Than Me', the breakout single and award-winning song, she outlined how frustrated she was with a partner who let her walk all over him. With lyrics that would now rightfully be called out for their insensitivities (the use of the word 'ladyboy' doesn't sit particularly well), she painted him as a limp squib. Later, on 'I Heard Love Is Blind', she sang remorselessly about cheating on a lover – reckoning that he shouldn't mind because the person she cheated with looked exactly like him. So what's the problem? 'Take the Box' was an almost word-for-word description of that car ride Janis had taken her on to deliver Chris's mementos back to him. These somewhat harsh sentiments were couched in such clever wordplay and shocking language, and wrapped up in such louche, irresistible music, that they became easy to overlook. Amy was a young woman comfortably outsassing the rest of the millennial pop crop. Her voice appealed to older listeners, her lyrics to younger ones. She had it covered.

Most die-hard Amy fans love *Frank*. They prefer its lighter touch to the tragic heartache of *Back to Black*, and the image of a young woman who's not afraid to be imperfectly behaved. It's an album that attempts to untangle the rat-king of thoughts in an adolescent brain. Traces of all the music Amy had grown up listening to can be found throughout it. Her voice might have the weight of hundreds of years of jazz icons behind it, but did any of them think to slip in a hip-hop beat or an RnB bassline? Did any of them think to write about the minutiae of a London teen's life? This was the magic of *Frank*. If Etta James had grown up listening to Thelonious Monk and sang the words from a Londoner's teenage diary, she might have come up with something like *Frank*.

Who else, in 2002, would open an album with a free-form jazz showboat? Jamie Cullum and Katie Melua were catering to an older easy-listening crowd – but Amy wasn't interested in pandering to Radio 2. She saw the great streaming genre mash-up coming; her music cannot be categorized as pure pop or pure jazz. It wasn't pure. It was messy, it was complicated, it referenced the past and influenced the future. It was *good*. There's not much in the way of ambiguity in Amy's music. She's not leaving the door ajar for you to interpret her meanings; when she's pissed off, she's pissed off; when she wants something from you, she'll tell you; and when she wants to sleep with another man, she will – as long as he looks like her boyfriend. It's like we're there with her, sitting in her bedroom surrounded by ashtrays and CDs, peering over her shoulder as she scribbles thoughts in her diary. We share in her process of figuring out the world. 'The vile, the ugly, the painful are not fit subjects for music', wrote Henry Krehbiel in 1897. Amy Winehouse would – we can only assume disrespectfully – disagree.

3

'I Do Drink a Lot, and I'm a Bad Drunk'

On 'Amy Amy Amy', the final track of *Frank*, Amy gives herself a strict talking to. It's like she's looking straight into the mirror and saying, 'You're never into the right guys'. Sure, in that case she was writing about a teacher driving her to distraction, but the point stood. She was attracted to men who were unattainable, inappropriate or the bad boy. It wasn't something that was about to change, even as she became famous and the power dynamic ought to have shifted even further in her favour.

Frank was out in the world and receiving mostly decent reviews from the British music press. Amy was playing shows, doing interviews and enjoying the first flushes of celebrity. She was known enough to be set apart from others, but not so famous that she couldn't go anywhere without being hassled. She and her friends would head out to the pubs around Camden almost every night, drinking, dancing and meeting boys as any 18-year-old would be. You'd find her in wrap dresses and pumps, big, obnoxious lipstick slicked across her lips, framing that wide, gap-toothed smile. Although she doesn't look particularly comfortable in her interviews from this time, she certainly doesn't look uncomfortable. Journalists found her spiky if she wasn't in the mood, or if they asked a question that she thought was stupid, but some were lucky enough to catch her in a good mood – expansive and open about the problems in her life and the things she wasn't happy with about her album. 'I don't care, I don't care in the least what people think about me. Never did, never will. Yes, as a result, I'm easy pickings because I am honest and unguarded. But life's too short to be worrying about that shit.' It's almost unheard of for a musician to bad-mouth their own release, especially on the promo trail when it's just come out. Maybe in 15 years' time, some will look back and go, 'Wow, why did no one stop me from trying to rap?', but very few will straight up say, especially to a journalist, 'I hate this bit'.

Interviews can be nerve-wracking situations for pop stars, particularly filmed interviews. But Amy Winehouse did not suffer fools gladly. Not certain kinds of fools anyway – some fools she suffered, nurtured, took to her heart and loved with a fierce loyalty. But the TV presenter who compared her to Dido was not one of these. Chewing her lip, those steady eyes that flash sometimes brown, sometimes green, stare intently at the offscreen interviewer, hardening infinitesimally as every word takes her another step further from Amy's approval. Watch the brows – they switch almost imperceptibly from neutral to nope. 'Look at Dido', the disembodied voice says – the eyebrows slip down ever so slightly. 'She used that album to clean out her emotional closet.' And now a full frown. 'Did she?', Amy says, making it very clear how she feels about that. Now the eyes have gone, sliding to the right as if to lock with a friend's.

'Are you hearing this?', she seems to say. 'Yeah! It's all about the breakdown of her relationship', the interviewer ploughs on. 'Well.' Amy is communicating her feelings with every iota of her being. The stiffened posture, the eyes sliding away from her questioner, the lip chewed with ever more intensity. 'I don't know about that.'

Would S Club 7 have thrown an apple at a Dido billboard? Would Daniel Bedingfield have chosen 'cat AIDS' over working with Katie Melua? Amy was a journalist's dream and nightmare all at once.

Of course, when Amy talked about things she didn't like about *Frank*, they weren't to do with her songwriting, nor her voice, which she knew was good and getting better. They were production decisions that she disagreed with – although whether she was there or gave her opinion as the decisions were made isn't clear at all. It's not hard to imagine that the production process would have bored Amy to tears. Fiddling around with the drum tone for hours on end, sitting in front of a screen and playing the tracks back over and over again. Doesn't that sound a bit like school? Doesn't it sound a bit like a 9 to 5 office job? So maybe she got bored and gave the thumbs up to finish off without her, or maybe she just didn't turn up that day. Either way, the result was a debut album that wasn't entirely the way she wanted it. 'I know what I want to do before the other person is even in the room. … Maybe in years to come I will be a good collaborator but at that point I was, like, Look, here is my music. We need brass on this, or that needs to be faster. And I don't want strings. If you want to work with me and you love strings, then go home', she said at the time. You can imagine her reaction when she heard the final masters of *Frank* and detected the strings rising and falling in the background. She wasn't happy with *Frank*, almost shrugging it off as she went. It was annoying but it was done. It was her first record – she'd know for next time.

She was also playing shows whenever and wherever she could. Being on stage wasn't much of a problem for Amy; her voice was good and she was confident in it. It was the second before actually being on stage that was the problem. The stepping out onto it. Adrenaline and nerves would course through her, sitting in the dressing room adjusting her hair or reapplying make-up; she found it very hard to get her nerve up. Dutch courage was always on hand and it became ritual – or habit – to swig at least one drink before she put herself in front of all those waiting ears. Other musicians have talked about the way performance can mess with your mind; the peaks and troughs, highs and lows of life on the road. One minute you're sitting alone in your dressing room with only your nerves for company, the next you're receiving near-constant adulation. And after the show, the congratulations, the attention: Amy thrived on attention, and this constant supply must have felt amazing, fulfilling in a way that she'd never experienced doing school performances or playing jazz clubs.

As newspapers began publishing stories and photos of Amy, her body image faltered. She'd always had a slightly precarious relationship with herself. As a teenager she'd said to her mum, 'Mum, I've got this great new diet: I eat what I want then I throw it up.' Followed by a cackle, it was always hard to tell the difference between hyperbole and reality with Amy. Janis recalls a red flag popping up in her mind, but not knowing whether to believe her outlandish daughter, who tended to say anything for a reaction. Obviously what Amy was describing was an eating disorder: bulimia nervosa. The more camera lenses that were on her, the more insecure she felt about her size, and although she was never formally diagnosed, she later talked about having had 'every eating disorder going'. Bulimia is a serious mental illness, and works in a cycle that is very difficult to break out of. Binge-eating followed by vomiting or fasting, followed by binge-eating, followed by more purging ... it can feel like an ideal fix for over-eating, or easier to disguise than starving yourself (anorexia), but it is just as dangerous and can lead to serious illness and death as the body fails to take on enough nutrients to function.

Amy lost several teeth in her twenties, a possible symptom of the illness – the enamel erodes due to frequent vomiting. As well as tooth damage, long-term bulimia can cause damage to the vocal cords and, more seriously, heart problems, both of which Amy ended up with, although the cause of each is by no means clear. Charities that help bulimia sufferers stress that early intervention offers the best chance of sustained recovery, but Amy was adept at hiding her problems with food and weight, even as she became rail thin. Fluctuating weight is another symptom of bulimia; even in the periods when Amy appeared to be a healthy weight, it could have been underpinned by this controlling condition. If she was suffering from bulimia, it must have felt as trapping as her drink and drug addictions. Amy always had a complicated relationship with control: she wanted it, but she didn't want it. She tended to surrender control when things got hard – to her family, to her partner (if they were up to the task), to her addictions. Eating disorders are not cured easily, quickly or without some cooperation from the sufferer. Perhaps bulimia became just another addiction on a list of things to deal with; perhaps Amy herself never wanted to stop badly enough to benefit from any help she was offered.

Regardless of the underlying causes, Amy's weight began to drop post-*Frank*.

'Stronger Than Me' had been the lead single from *Frank*. Although it didn't really make any impact on the charts (in fact, none of *Frank*'s singles broke the Top 40 in the UK), it was recognized in a way that meant much more to Amy. Its inventive melding of pop melodies, jazz vocals and hip-hop beats won Amy the 2004 Ivor Novello Award for Best Contemporary Song, beating Kylie Minogue's song 'Slow' and Dizzee Rascal's 'Jus' a Rascal'. Of all the awards she won in her lifetime, this was the one she was most proud of. Rather than a popularity contest or a political statement, winning an Ivor Novello sets you apart as a master of the songwriting craft. Of course, she rocked up to the ceremony an hour late and nearly missed the opportunity to receive the award herself. 'I have to write honestly about things which happen to me', she said in her acceptance speech, 'and hope people can relate to that.' Sometime later she turned up at Janis's house with a heavy bag. She casually reached in, pulled out the statue and said, 'This is for you, Mum.'

Janis, meanwhile, had been having more health issues. She'd been free of MS symptoms for many years, but in 2003 she caught a viral infection that landed her in hospital for a week. She was having terrible dizzy spells, so to try to find out why, her doctors gave her an MRI scan. 'It was found I had lesions on the brain', she told the *Irish Times*. 'It was then finally confirmed that I have secondary progressive MS.' It was bad news but Janis was, ironically, a little relieved to finally have an explanation – that these minor issues in fact added up to something major. 'I could start to live with it and deal with it', she said.

After the flurry of activity around *Frank* (and a post-Ivors sales boost), everyone expected Amy to set about writing album number two. That's not quite what happened. Instead of knuckling down (which, as we know, is not something Amy excelled at), she set about enjoying the freedom of financial security, and Camden as her own personal playground. She became a regular at the Hawley Arms, shooting pool, smoking untold numbers of Marlboro Reds and flirting with the regulars. One day a tall, lanky guy in a pork pie hat caught her eye. Blake Fielder-Civil was a classic indie kid, commanding attention easily and living like there was no tomorrow. Blake had a girlfriend already, but that didn't matter much to the woman who'd written 'I Heard Love Is Blind' – and anyway, she had never been backward about going forward with men she liked the look of. It didn't seem to matter much to Blake either.

Blake was 22 at the time. He'd dropped out of school in Lincolnshire and moved to London, where he was working casually as a gopher on music video shoots and tending bar between video gigs. He was in a wild crowd of indie lads who spent their evenings getting high and causing trouble around Amy's usual Camden haunts. Blake was handsome in a kind of ratty way. His cheekbones jutted in a way that was very in vogue, and there was a hint of drugginess about the dark eyes, the gaunt face, the long, thin legs. Amy had begun her tattoo collection, and Blake's scrapbook of topless dolly girls and names through hearts no doubt influenced the line drawings and vintage-style sailor tattoos that Amy became known for. Blake dressed in skin-tight jeans and a rotating wardrobe of loose-fitting shirts and faded, moth-eaten T-shirts. Even when he didn't have a roll-up hanging out of the corner of his mouth, there was something about him that implied a roll-up wasn't far from his person at any time. He tried to cultivate an air of superiority and it worked, his smile often accompanied by a calculated flash in the eyes; he was handsome, in demand and he knew it. What better boost to the ego of a young video assistant with an inflated sense of his own importance in Camden at the height of the indie scene than to date a bona fide celebrity? Who better than a smitten, insecure young woman to bankroll his burgeoning drug habit?

We should be generous and suppose that Fielder-Civil never intended to use Amy Winehouse. And we should also acknowledge that Amy seemed – at first, anyway – quite happy to be used by him. Maybe it started out as a laugh with his mates – he has a face you can imagine saying,

'Here, bet I can shag her' over his fifth pint of beer – but there are photos of the two of them in those early days of their relationship that look almost idyllic. Rolling about in the park with bedhead, walking to the pub with Blake's protective arm slung easily around Amy's shoulders: there was always an implication that they had just come from a scrappy, vigorous round in the bedroom. What did they talk about during those golden hours together? How many texts did they send when they were apart? At what point did Amy sense Blake pulling away from her, and when did she come to the cold, hard realization that she'd lost him?

The one thing we know for sure is the soundtrack to this relationship. Pub jukeboxes pumping out sixties girl groups like The Shangri-Las and The Ronettes, playing into the couple's retro style and probably colouring Amy's memories of that time in a comforting soft-focus sepia that smoothed out all the rough edges. But boy, those edges were rough. Their relationship was very intense and very messy. Amy was obsessed with the new man in her life, adapting to his likes and dislikes as many of us do when we meet someone new. But rather than, say, feigning an interest in a certain type of music to impress a boy, Amy switched up her substance intake. By her own admission in 2007, 'He doesn't smoke weed, so I started drinking more and not smoking as much.' She'd already been using alcohol as a crutch to help her get on stage and perform, but now she was drinking to excess when she was around Blake, which, during that tempestuous time, was a lot.

Amy's parents didn't meet Blake this time around, but they certainly heard enough about him. From Amy, yes, but also from the press, who were very taken with their public displays of affection and drunkenness. Amy's behaviour changed around Blake as well – here at last was a man who exerted the kind of power and control she'd craved, a man who withheld his affections just enough to keep her interested. He was also trouble with a capital T. He'd lord it up in expensive bars, buying drinks for a coterie of hangers-on and gesture to Amy, saying, 'Don't worry, she's paying.' He was open about his extra-curricular drug habits and invited drug dealers to her flat, forging connections that it would later be near-impossible for her to break. She, in turn, became a different person around Blake; cutesy and flirty, as she had been her whole life, but now also looking to him for validation, almost permission, with everything she said.

Her style, too, was evolving. The scratchy tattoos she'd begun investing in grew in number and intricacy, and her new thin frame spurred her to wear as little as possible, as if to show off the maximum amount of skin that she could get away with. She'd wear her tiny shorts unbuttoned, and kids' size T-shirts that sat like crop tops. It was a far cry from the 18-going-on-30-something style she'd been partial to around the making of *Frank*.

After seven intense months, Blake broke up with Amy. Theirs had been a tempestuous relationship and Amy for her part later regretted the way she had treated Blake. It wasn't long before Amy found out he'd gone back to the woman he'd been with when he met her. This was the first big crack in Amy's heart. She was bereft. Her confidence was shaken. It didn't matter that her friends and family were all relieved to have seen the back of him. No matter that they told her he was bad news, a bad guy, not worth it, she deserved better – if she deserved better, why didn't he want her? 'I thought we'd never see each other again', she told the BBC in 2008. 'I wanted to die.'

4

'Didn't Matter, Got a Good Song Out of It'

I t's a myth that great art can only come from great pain – but it's true that a bit of pain can help things along. Amy was devastated by the break-up with Blake. She was dating other people, but her heart and her mind were still on the man she'd been with for those seven shining months. She'd been so in love but was also plagued by the memory of how badly they'd treated each other: the screaming rows, the poisonous barbs, the crippling hangovers. Heartbreak is a kind of grief, and she was deep in it. Knowing that he'd gone back to his ex-girlfriend was making the pain even harder to bear.

Amy was writing bits and pieces of songs, but it was now well over a year since *Frank* had come out and her label were anxious for her to get going on her second LP. But Amy just wouldn't – possibly couldn't – work. She spent her days in a fog of wine and vodka, playing The Shangri-Las' 'I Can Never Go Home Anymore' over and over again. 'When me and my boyfriend finished, I used to listen to that song on repeat, just sitting on my kitchen floor with a bottle of Jack Daniel's. I'd pass out, wake up and do it again. My flatmate used to come in, leave bags of KFC and just leave. She'd be like: there's your dinner, I'm going out. It's the saddest song in the world.' Her weight continued to plummet. Her management company and label had left her to her own devices between records, possibly assuming she was writing songs as well as getting papped and partying. But by spring 2005, it was clear that something had to give.

'I was in a bad way', she later told the *Daily Record*. She knew she was drinking too much, even with her proudly won high tolerance for alcohol – 'I was definitely drinking too much … The kinds of states I was getting myself into was a joke. I'll admit it was a joke.' At first, drinking had just been 'something to do', as she'd told *GQ*, but now it was something else. Friends would meet her in the early evening and find her already trashed after an afternoon of drinking alone, topping up whatever was left in her system from the previous evening. 'I'd be wrecked from the day before, having stayed up all night and I'd still be up.' Of course, given Amy's tendency to walk a fine line between two opposing states, it was half shamefaced admission, and half a brag.

Amy wasn't a great drunk. She could be a lot of fun, unleashing her whip-sharp wit on unsuspecting strangers, but the old bully could resurface, too. The one that made enemies of her classmates and inspired fear among her friends. 'I do drink a lot, and I'm a bad drunk, a very violent drunk', she told the *Irish Times* in 2006. To *GQ* the same year she admitted, 'I am difficult if I'm drinking. I can be a cruel person. If I have 20 units, I can get violent, particularly if I am unhappy.' She'd been talking about a recent incident in which she punched a fan in the face: the girl had come up to Amy and her then boyfriend, fellow musician Alex Clare, in the pub. She'd gushed to Amy about how much she loved her music and kissed her on the cheek, but then turned to Alex and said, 'She's fucked.' Regardless of the accuracy of the statement, Amy saw red. She punched the girl and then, as he tried to calm her down, punched Alex too. It wasn't the first time she'd been violent with her partner. From the *Irish Times* again: 'With Alex, he will bring it up the following day when I've sobered up. It really embarrasses me to hear I've punched him in the face six times. Again.' Amy's skewed vision of gender roles allowed her to let herself off. 'It does make me want to cut down on the booze. I really do try not to drink, but I'm a very self-destructive person. I keep saying to [Alex] that he can take it. I'm a little girl, he's a big guy.'

It was clear that Amy was in trouble and that she couldn't carry on in this way. She'd have to find a way through the heartbreak – and her management thought that the way to do this was to stop drinking (or at the very least cut down). Her old friend Tyler James had suggested this too, and between them, the idea of going to rehab was floated. You probably know how this story goes – it forms the basis of her 2006 mega-hit of the same name. Although she obviously knew, in hindsight at least, that she needed some kind of help, Amy did not like the idea of rehab. She didn't like people to probe her, to uncover things about her that she'd kept hidden for years – perhaps since her parents' divorce, perhaps since her first problems with food, perhaps even earlier than that, from wherever her deep-seated insecurities had stemmed. The tragedy of the break-up with Blake was so fantastically overblown, such a soap opera of reaction, it had tipped her over the edge. But she asked her dad, who was active in her career and management at this point, what he thought. He didn't quite say, 'You're fine', but he didn't push her. 'I asked my dad if he thought I needed to go. He said no but I should give it a try. So I did.'

To be fair to her, she did give it a try. But can we truly class 15 minutes with a counsellor a solid 'try'? Amy told the *Sun* in 2006, 'I went in, said hello and explained that I drink because I am in love and have fucked up the relationship. Then I walked out.' In fact, the session was a little bit more in depth than that; the counsellor asked if she thought she was an alcoholic, to which she answered, 'Maybe – I didn't want to say no because he might think I'm in denial.' He then tried to talk to her about alcoholism, and what treatment could look like and what she could expect from the process, but bored Amy from the back of the classroom kicked back in. 'I kind of switched off and 15 minutes later I went, "Thanks very much" and walked out.'

It shouldn't come as a huge surprise that therapy didn't work for Amy. It was too much sitting still and being told to do something in a concentrated way. That's not how she worked – she preferred to fly by the seat of her pants, scribbling notes here and there, creating something from hundreds of tiny shards. In the studio she could concentrate because she was singing, her one great love, but sitting in a therapist's office? Staying in a residential rehab facility? She'd be like a caged tiger. 'Some people go to rehab and treat it like Butlins', she later said. 'Some people go because they think it will really sort them out and it does. But me, I'm from the school which believes that you can only sort yourself out, you can't rely on other people to sort out your problems.' So rehab was out of the question: if anyone was going to get Amy through this period, it was Amy herself.

She was, she said later, clinically depressed during this period. The songs that she dragged out of her broken heart and her sluggish brain are ripe with the pain she was going through – and the fact that she managed to write them all is something to be applauded. Depression takes everything away – motivation, joy, energy, will to live. Couple that with near-constant drunkenness and you don't exactly have a recipe for the perfect creative conditions. Although, listening to *Back to Black*, perhaps you do. 'I have to feel very strongly about something before I can write about it. But when I start, I'm on a roll.'

The year 2005 had been a rough one. Amy was tired, broken and only just starting to pull herself up from rock bottom. She felt like she needed a fresh start: to clean house, to start over. At the time, her contract with her managers at Brilliant 19 was coming to an end and she decided that, instead of continuing on with Nick Shymansky and Nick Godwyn, she'd find a new manager to work with. She suspected she had some good songs under her belt from what she'd written over those long, painful months, and she already had ideas to move away from the hip-hop-tinged jazz sound of *Frank*. Plus, no doubt, she was still smarting from 19's attempts to get her to stop drinking. It felt like the right time for a fresh start. So she moved on.

She decided to hire Raye Cosbert as her new manager; Raye had been a concert promoter and had never managed an artist before Amy. But she got on well with him and he seemed to have some kind of authority with her. He was physically huge compared to the tiny Amy and perhaps that was appealing, as though he gave her a sense of security. Guy Moot of EMI once said that there had been two pivotal moments in Amy's career – when she met Raye Cosbert, and when she met Mark Ronson.

After years of messing about, drinking, partying and falling apart, *Back to Black* only took Amy about six months to write in the end. The songs were good, and the ideas for how they should sound were solid. But it took another major relationship in Amy's life to really get things cracking. In 2005, Island Records' Darcus Beese introduced her to a young DJ and producer called Mark Ronson. Ronson had released one album by that point, a record full of party tunes and famous rappers, the kind of surface-level pop music that Amy loathed. She wasn't exactly thrilled at the idea of meeting him, but she went along with it (thanks partly to the soothing presence of her new manager, who smoothed her relationship with Island and made her feel more comfortable about moving forward with the album).

Mark Ronson is a tall, good-looking man with a trans-atlantic accent, thanks to a childhood split between London and New York. Amy warmed to him almost instantly, his easy manner and shared musical interests with hers easing the way – not to mention they were both Jewish Londoners, which gave them an easy shorthand and shared experience. Janis later referred to Mark Ronson as 'another of Amy's brothers'. Ronson was another calming presence in this new chapter of Amy's life and career, and he instinctively knew what the record needed for it to have the vintage, sixties girl group feel that Amy wanted to channel. They flew to New York to record in his studio, using vintage fifties equipment that gives *Back to Black* its full, warm feel.

The songs Amy had written were all about her relationship and break-up with Blake. She and Ronson worked to polish them up together – Amy would play him a bit of a song she'd been working on, or send him a song she couldn't stop listening to, and he'd mull it over, then come back to her with ideas of how to incorporate it into the record they were making. They exchanged songs by countless artists: Motown records, The Angels, Leonard Cohen, Earl Carroll and the Cadillacs. 'We … just started talking the way music geeks do when they get together', Amy told *Rolling Stone* in 2007. They wrote 'Rehab' together almost instinctively – 'I sang the hook – I sang it as a joke', Amy told *Paper* magazine in February 2007. 'Mark started laughing and saying "That's so funny, that's so funny, Amy. Whose song is that, man?" I told him, "I just wrote it off the top of my head, I was just joking." And he said, "It would be so cool if you had a whole song about rehab." I said, "Well I could write it right now. Let's go to the studio." And that was it.'

Over 11 short songs she painstakingly dissected the feelings and actions that had led to this point. It must have been hard for Amy to relive those songs day after day in the sound-proof booth where she laid down her vocals. To access the part of her that was fragile, only a bottle of wine away from completely falling apart again. She often had a drink in the booth with her – a rum and coke or a Southern Comfort and lemonade – but she was turning up to work every day, and the vocals she was laying down were nothing short of astonishing. They spent three weeks recording in New York, mostly with live instruments to capture that Motown feel, and then Ronson was left to slot everything else into place.

Ronson wasn't the only producer on *Back to Black* – Amy's old friend and collaborator on *Frank*, Salaam Remi, was also involved in some of the tracks. Quite a departure from cosmopolitan New York, Amy went back down to his home in Miami to work on the songs. It seems funny to think of these heart-rending tracks being created in sunny Florida – the tragic, funereal air completely at odds with Bermuda shorts, spring breakers and retirees chasing the winter sun. Miami's music scene is much more club-orientated, more Pitbull than Piaf, but Salaam had amassed a huge amount of equipment in order to figure out the vintage sound for Amy – they called his studio the 'instrument zoo'. Unlike on *Frank*, where Amy lost interest and left others to put the record together (which resulted in those infamous strings), *Back to Black* holds together because she was so sure of how she wanted it to sound. Remi and his engineers spent hours tuning snare drums to get the right sixties sound, experimenting with microphone set-ups and tinkering until they found the tone that Amy was shooting for.

It's strange to go back and try to listen to *Back to Black* with new ears. It's become such a part of the cultural landscape that even if you've never listened to the full album, you know parts of it intimately – in the same way that even if you've never seen *Star Wars*, you know something about Luke Skywalker and his family situation. It's also very hard to listen to now you know it's part of the end of the story, rather than the opening chapter it should have been. So much of what Amy went through in life is in there. She snuck stories of a 20-something's occasionally scandalous love life into the living rooms and CD players of millions of parents by couching talk of wet dicks, carpet burn, too much booze and general 'fuckery' in vintage Motown sounds and girl-group melodies. A Trojan horse with a capital T. As usual, it's full of feints and misdirection – 'Rehab', for example, a party tune we spend our Saturday nights dancing to, but also immortalizing a turning point, a moment in time when maybe an addict who later died could have been saved. The crab-claw beat and jaunty horns belie what we now know was a life or death subject matter – but hey, it's also a killer pop song. And sometimes you can listen to it one way, and sometimes the other.

The homages to the olden days extend to the album's length – 11 songs, each around the 3-minute mark, as if they're set to be released on '45s, so it's a short but bittersweet trip through heartache and out into … what? Redemption? Resolution? Resignation? Perhaps a bit of all three – but certainly not into rehabilitation. Just as with *Frank*, Amy lambasts herself for making bad choices. 'You Know I'm No Good' shrugs to us like, 'Hey, you knew this wouldn't end well.' These songs burn with Amy's fear that she'll always be left, alone, crying on the kitchen floor with a cold bag of KFC by her side.

'Me & Mr Jones' has an all-time great opening line, featuring Amy's favourite word: 'fuckery'. Even when she's angry, Amy is only ever capable of being Amy. The jazz-club snare, the moody brass, the sweetness of the way she sings the title line. She's angry but resigned. She's sad but she's open to forgiveness. It doesn't sound like something made in the new millennium – it sounds adrift in space and time, anchored by that voice.

And, of course, there's the emotional gut punch of the title track, almost Sisyphean in its structure, as though we are doomed to repeat the cycle over and over. He'll go back to her; Amy will go back to black. The doomiest-sounding tambourine slaps since The Shangri-Las, and the pounding, discordant piano riff like a racing heart – she's in full mourning. It's no surprise that the video for 'Back to Black' was shot in a cemetery; there's a funereal air to it, the grief and loss of a relationship breakdown. You don't need to know much about Amy and Blake's relationship to spot the details that relate to it – the lover going back 'to her' while the singer sinks deeper into oblivion. It's not a howl of pain but a sob into a cushion, a brave face trying to assert itself. That church bell tolling near the end as Amy sings 'black' over and over; the oblivion of it all. How can she go on from here? It is devastating. What other song of the 2000s has this power?

Back to Black was released on 27 October 2006 in the UK, but it wasn't until the following year that things went stratospheric: it sold over 1.85 million copies, becoming the best-selling album of 2007. Unlike *Frank*, *Back to Black* also got a US release, entering the Billboard charts at number 7 and becoming the highest debut for a UK female of all time. It was a smash, catapulting Amy into the upper echelons of the A-list and all the flashbulbs and demands on her time that came with it.

5

'Drugs Are for Mugs'

As she geared up to head out on the *Back to Black* promo trail, Amy seemed to be making healthy new choices. She was seeing Alex Clare and she'd thrown herself into a new workout regime, heading to the gym six afternoons a week. Preferring to work out surrounded by men rather than women, who she sensed were judging her, these gym sessions were often carried out in a full face of make-up. The image of Amy pounding away on the treadmill with eyeliner and sweat running down her cheeks or pumping iron in a pair of heeled pumps is amusing, but she took the whole thing seriously. She toned up and slimmed down, trying once again to exert control over her body.

But she was still drinking. As 'Rehab' was released as the first single from the album in October, Amy was booked on *The Charlotte Church Show* to promote it. She turned up, got bored and spent all the hanging around time that goes with TV shooting in the green room drinking. Although she seemed quite steady at the start of the show, by the time she and Charlotte performed their grand finale (a duet of Michael Jackson's 'Beat It'), Amy was a mess. It's a truly dreadful performance. Amy wanders about the stage looking dazed, beehive askew. When she sings those rhythmic, pulsing verses she's so far off the beat you can barely even tell what song it is, and as she slurs her way towards the chorus she rarely finds the melody. Charlotte Church desperately tries to hold the whole thing together as the camera finds any opportunity to shoot away from Amy, lingering on the guitarist soloing for what feels like a decade. It's like 2 am in a karaoke bar, not the finale of a prime-time television show. According to the *Daily Mirror*'s report at the time, that shambles of a performance took three takes. Charlotte Church later said that Amy's problem was she kept forgetting the words – 'I told Amy, when I squeeze you it's your turn to sing. We did the whole thing with me poking her in the back.'

Janis was horrified. Mitch had his head in his hands. Amy's label was worried. But Amy was unabashed and unrepentant. When interviewed by *Scotland on Sunday* a few weeks later, the reporter tells her that *The Charlotte Church Show* performance had been bordering on incomprehensible. 'She just laughs and tells me she can't wait to see it.'

Unfortunately, it wasn't the only time Amy's drunken antics created an iconic piece of television. In November 2006, she took part in the music panel show *Never Mind the Buzzcocks*, hosted by Simon Amstell. His was an acerbic wit that could bring down even the biggest of egos, but Amy and Simon had met before – when he was at Channel 4's *Popworld* they'd toured the streets of London in a black cab, canvassing members of the public for votes in the BRITs. It had culminated with Amy throwing apples at a huge billboard for Dido's album. They clearly had a similar sensibility when it came to celebrity and got on as a result.

But as the quiz wore on, it became increasingly clear that Amy was trashed. When she asked for more vodka in her *Never Mind the Buzzcocks* mug, Amstell feigned horror that was probably based in something real, and at the news that Amy was meeting up with Pete Doherty (the singer of The Libertines and well-known drug addict) he cried out, 'He wants to sell you drugs! Don't go near him! Do something with Katie Melua instead, there you go.' Amy leaned back in her chair, pushed her hair over her shoulder and said, 'I'd rather have cat AIDS, thank you.'

Amstell wasn't about to let the rumours of Amy's drug abuse go as a subject. When she jokingly referred to an odd sound she made standing up as 'my new thing', he said, 'Is it? I thought that was crack.' Later, having spat some water over her shoulder, Simon ribbed her mercilessly. 'Let it die, please. Let it die … Please', she groaned. 'The addiction I'd like to die', he told her. 'This isn't even a pop quiz anymore. It's an intervention, Amy.' That wasn't even the most prescient line in the show. The part that stayed with Janis, watching in horror at home, felt like an omen.

'We used to be close', Amstell told her, jokingly.

'We were close, but she's dead.'

'Can we resuscitate the old Winehouse? I loved you when you were sober.'

'She's dead.'

In 2009, the BBC released a DVD compilation of the best bits of *Never Mind the Buzzcocks*. It was during a time when Amy seemed to be in recovery and on it, Simon Amstell provides a commentary. He talks about this episode slightly shamefacedly, saying, 'It wouldn't have been funny if she'd died. But she didn't, so it's funny again.' Bill Bailey, the comedian whose team Amy had been on, told *NME* in 2015 that he can no longer listen to 'Love Is a Losing Game'; the tragedy of it all is too much.

But at the time, these antics gave Amy the air of a rock'n'roll icon; they were entertaining to watch and hear about, and the papers knew it. It seemed terribly glamorous to act without conscience or consequence. It's almost impossible to imagine the level of media scrutiny Amy came under at this time. Tabloid newspapers are always looking for something explosive and controversial to put on their front pages, and Amy's troubles always sold well. Paparazzi would camp outside her house at all hours of the day and night, meaning that she could barely pop out for a pint of milk without it making the next day's edition. It helped that her look had completely morphed from Topshop sale-rack to rockabilly bad girl with a sixties slant. Her hair was now teased into a towering beehive (with the help of a wig or two), and her eyeliner, which had always been heavily applied, was now a hard flash of black across her lids, a whoosh stretching to her brow line. The heavy make-up and overwhelming hair made her facial features seem smaller and her body at its thinnest seem tiny and fragile.

When she spoke about her make-up, she danced around describing it as warpaint – it wasn't, not really, it was more of a mask. Something to hide behind. 'I think I need my hair to be big', she told *Paper* magazine. 'It gives me confidence; it's like a big woven security blanket.' The more insecure Amy felt on the inside, the sharper the eyeliner, the bigger the wig. She had a closet full of wigs in her flat, which her mum referred to as her 'litter of wigs', to match her sizeable collection of cats. Likewise, her trademark ballet slippers seemed to breed, tumbling mismatched out of a cupboard in her room. Her wardrobe was stocked with fitted Fred Perry polo shirts and waist-cinching dresses, and she favoured towering heels when she took to the stage (although she often kicked them off halfway through the performance). Her tattoos spread from a smattering to a sleeve's worth, with the most notable being a topless woman, the words 'Daddy's girl', Cynthia's name in a heart (of which the lady in question stridently did not approve) and a buttoned-down pocket over her heart, with the name Blake above it. Her look was so different to any other mid-millennial pop star that it instantly became iconic – during her troubled years and beyond, to dress as Amy Winehouse became a bad taste Halloween tradition for some.

In May 2006, Cynthia died. Amy was distraught. Cynthia had been one of the few people in life that Amy had really looked up to, and one of even fewer who could exert any kind of discipline over her. She and Amy had remained close even as Amy's life went off the rails, and losing her was a big blow.

Although the promo trail had been full of ups and downs (a particular highlight being Amy heckling at the Q Awards, telling Bono to fuck off, which, let's face it, we've all dreamed of doing), *Back to Black* was flying out the door. The relentless press Amy was enduring probably didn't hurt sales, but when the song 'Back to Black' came out, everything changed. At the start of 2007 it climbed up the UK charts to number one – and, more than that, it was almost inescapable.

'Rehab', 'Tears Dry on Their Own' and 'Back to Black' played on constant rotation on the radio, in shops, at the peak of indie discos and tinnily emanated from headphones on the bus; the album was *everywhere*. Amy was no longer just another BRIT School alumnus enjoying a reasonable flush of success: Amy Winehouse was a star. 'Are you proud of me, Dad?', she asked Mitch at the party they threw to celebrate her hitting number one. Of course he was.

It can't have been easy for Alex Clare. As Amy's current boyfriend he had to suffer through the wild success of her record full of songs all about how much she loved her ex-boyfriend. He was the polar opposite of Blake: stocky, bearded, rational. He'd been a big cheese at Radio 1 and now worked for Amy's label, EMI. It wasn't really easy for anyone close to Amy to listen to *Back to Black*, having seen what she'd been through to wrestle it into being. Mitch writes in his book: 'It occurred to me recently that one of the biggest-selling UK albums of the twenty-first century so far is about the biggest low-life scumbag that God ever put breath into. Quite ironic, isn't it?'

As the new year dawned and the album shot up the charts, Alex suspected that Amy and Blake had been seeing each other again. He also thought that Amy had started taking drugs; although there had been rumours in the newspapers by this point, no one in Amy's circle truly believed she would take anything harder than marijuana. She'd had a saying in the early days of her career that she'd chant at gigs, 'Class A drugs are for mugs'. But Alex was concerned enough to go to Mitch and tell him that he thought Amy had been smoking heroin. He said he could smell it on her.

Tyler James had also warned Mitch that Blake was into hard drugs, but with no evidence to suggest Amy had been seduced by them, he shrugged it off.

Amy and Alex broke up in early 2007 and things were officially over one day in Camden when Clare went to the Hawley Arms for a drink. He and Amy had often been found in there – it was one of their regular haunts. It was also the place where Amy and Blake had become synonymous with each other. He ordered a pint, sat down and then went pale. He couldn't believe what he was seeing – Amy, his very recent ex-girlfriend, wrapped around that tall, skinny, rat-faced ex of hers. At the time, he wrote on his Myspace profile: 'After turning up at 3am at The Hawley Arms I saw the ex with her ex and I saw red mist. I was shaking like a leaf and decided to get leathered while she sat there inebriated and on the lap of her ex. I'm skint, heartbroken and homeless. Bad luck comes in threes, as the old saying goes, but shit, what's a man to do?' The Alex and Amy show was over; the Amy and Blake show was back on.

It had taken surprisingly little time for Blake to re-emerge into Amy's life. This time, he said, he was completely unattached and hers for good. Amy was thrilled and her dormant obsession with Blake resurfaced. Her family noted the timing – Blake had dumped her when her career seemed to have stalled and come running back the minute she was back in the limelight. But Amy didn't notice, or if she did, she didn't care. Any second away from Blake was a second wasted, in her mind. She insisted that he was included in all conversations whether they were personal, business or other. If you called Amy and she was with Blake, either she wouldn't answer, or she'd answer but she'd be so distracted by his presence that it was hardly worth trying to talk to her.

Neither of her parents had met Blake by this point. She finally introduced Blake to Mitch in a stilted though pleasant meeting at Amy's new Jeffrey's Place flat in Camden. Blake was on best behaviour, shaking hands, talking about his career, such as it was, and although he was a bit scruffy and thin, Mitch left feeling like his daughter was happy and Alex Clare's accusations of drug use had been born of jealousy. It was almost as if Amy disappeared into this new being: not Amy anymore but Blake's Bird. Her vocabulary for talking about him changed too; she'd refer to him as 'my man' and use language that her family and friends didn't recognize as her own. 'It was like she was some kind of gangster's moll', Janis despaired, thinking it both silly and worrying that the daughter she knew seemed to be disappearing entirely.

One day in May 2007, Amy and Blake disappeared off to Miami together. Miami had a special place in Janis's heart – she had family there and she'd travelled to the city alone as a teenager, which had been a very formative experience. She and Amy had also been to Miami together when Amy was a teenager; it felt like their place, a place of self-discovery and reinvention. So when Amy called Janis giggling and told her that she and Blake had just got married, alone, without any family around them, in Janis and Amy's special place, Janis felt utterly betrayed. Not only had she been deprived of the opportunity to attend her only daughter's wedding, but she'd married a man Janis didn't know or trust in a place that seemed designed to hurt her. Mitch was angry with Amy too, more on Janis's behalf than his own. Over a series of heated transatlantic phone calls with his daughter, he got the impression that Blake had steered her into marrying without any of her family present. Although he still believed that if Blake was into drugs, his daughter would bully him out of it, he was starting to worry about Blake's influence. 'They'd been married five minutes and he'd already put my back up.'

'We'll have a huge party when we get back', Amy promised, but it did little to settle the unease of either of her parents and the party never happened. Mitch and Janis both remembered the pain and torment Amy had gone through after her break-up with Blake – an obsessive, co-dependent relationship was not healthy for their daughter, given her addictive personality.

The first terrifying indication that something was wrong with Amy's health came that summer. It was a warm, showery evening in August and Amy and Blake were alone at Amy's flat in Jeffrey's Place. Suddenly Amy went pale and collapsed, her body jerking involuntarily on the floor. Blake panicked. This had never happened before. He wrestled her into the recovery position and then, for some reason, instead of calling an ambulance, he phoned Amy's close friend Juliette. She drove over from Barnet to take Amy to hospital, where they arrived at about 1 am. It was close to an hour after Amy first fell ill. Mitch arrived 15 minutes later to find Blake gone and Amy woozy and incoherent after having her stomach pumped. No medical conclusions were drawn but, at a hasty meeting the next morning, Mitch, Raye and Nick Shymansky worried that it was caused by the amount Amy had been drinking. Later, it turned out that it wasn't just alcohol to blame. A lab report showed that she'd had a buffet of drugs in her system: heroin, cocaine, ketamine and marijuana. Blake, talking to the *News of the World* in 2008, confirmed it: 'We had been taking drugs all day long – heroin and crack. Then my wife, who I love with all my heart and soul, just started shaking violently in front of me.'

The denial that the family had been in about Amy's substance abuse was shattered. They had steadfastly chosen to believe that the press had it in for Amy, that she was 'just' drinking, that it was only Blake who had potentially been using hard drugs. Amy's old saying that 'Class A drugs are for mugs' no longer held true – or if it did, it confirmed Amy as the mug. No one was in any doubt about where the drugs had originated from, so it became important to keep Amy away from Blake for the time being. Mitch booked her a room at the Four Seasons Hotel in Surrey, inviting Juliette and another close friend, Lauren Gilbert, along to make her feel more at home. There had been no sign of Blake at the hospital since he and Juliette dropped Amy off and when Amy was discharged the next day, and as far as anyone knew, he hadn't even called to see how his wife was. This was suspicious, but his lack of care could be a good thing: at least he wouldn't know where Amy was going. Or so they thought.

Later that day, as Amy, Juliette and Lauren settled into the hotel, Mitch, Nick and Raye talked about what to do next. Janis and Amy's brother Alex lived too far away to make it worth them visiting the hospital before Amy was discharged, but they arrived at the hotel that afternoon. Janis describes walking up to Amy's room, saying 'the world seemed to shift into slow motion'. 'She was skeletal, like something out of Belsen concentration camp. Hunched over the bed, she was sitting with a white towel wrapped around her. I could see the scars on her arms where she'd cut herself. She was like an apparition.' Janis was so terrified she could barely speak as Amy clutched her and said over and over, 'Mummy, Mummy, I'm so sorry, Mummy.' It was Alex's voice that rang through the brittle tension of the hotel room. He was wild with anger and fear, livid with his sister for playing so fast and loose with her life. 'You're going to kill yourself', he shouted at her. 'You're not going to live to 25, you know that, don't you?' It was crystal clear to everyone that Amy was an addict, and even as Alex told her bluntly that she needed to go to rehab, she snapped back, 'No.'

It seemed futile to try to reason with her: even this episode hadn't shaken her enough to make her want to seek help. That theory was proved by her next visitor: Blake. At some point Amy had managed to call him and tell him where she was. He sauntered up to her room at about 10 pm, and by 11 pm Mitch was suitably worried about Amy's behaviour ('wasn't her usual self … talking a lot of nonsense') that he called a doctor to see her. After a quick examination, the doctor told Mitch that Amy had just taken something – he suspected crack cocaine – and that if she went on using she could have another seizure. He added that the danger of death was very real.

By this time the hotel was crawling with reporters and photographers. News of Amy's seizure had spread, and everyone was hoping for a glimpse of the patient.

Amy with best friend Juliette Ashby in their teenage years.

Amy poses in front of the Hog's Head pub on Camden Parkway in February 2003, eight months before the release of *Frank*.

TOP – Amy performing with her friend Tyler James in 2004.

ABOVE – A fresh new face on the UK music scene,
Amy is photographed for the *Observer* in 2004.

Amy arrives at the ceremony for the 2004 Mercury Music Prize,
for which *Frank* is nominated.

Two years later, the change in Amy's personal style is notable as she performs at the Forum, Kentish Town, in November 2006.

ABOVE – As *Back to Black* receives mounting acclaim,
Amy arrives at the South Bank Awards in January 2007.

OPPOSITE – Amy performs at the 2007 BRIT Awards (top), and is congratulated
by manager Raye Cosbert as she wins Best British Female Solo Artist (bottom).

Amy at the Isle of Wight festival in July 2007 with husband Blake Fielder-Civil; the reunited couple had married without any family present two months earlier.

Pursued by the paparazzi: in March 2007 (top), and on her way to visit Blake in Pentonville Prison in December that same year (bottom).

After a year of highs and lows, Amy performs at the 2008 BRIT Awards with *Back to Black* producer and friend, Mark Ronson.

With dad Mitch (top) and mum Janis (bottom) at her live-feed performance for the Grammys at Hammersmith's Riverside Studios, February 2008.

On stage at the concert held for Nelson Mandela's
ninetieth birthday, June 2008.

Amy is photographed during a break in her trial for assault
at Westminster Magistrates Court on 23 July 2009.

Amy meets her hero Tony Bennett backstage after his concert
at London's Royal Albert Hall in July 2010.

Amy is immortalized alongside other members of the '27 Club' in a mural painted by Eduardo Kobra on New York City's Lower East Side.

To make matters worse, Blake's parents had arrived and were adamant that all the problems stemmed from Amy: they didn't think Blake had a problem, wouldn't accept that he could be to blame for anything. As tempers flared, Blake's stepfather, Giles Civil, ended up in a screaming match with Mitch on the hotel terrace. Amy's doctor recommended that the couple try a stint at the Causeway Retreat on Osea Island. Located on the east coast of the UK, the island that hosted the facility was an hour's drive out of London, and because it was an island that was only accessible by road for about an hour a day, everyone hoped they wouldn't be able to have any drugs smuggled to them. There was no Daddy saying she's fine this time – Mitch was leading the charge. There were signs that Amy wanted to get clean and find a way back to a functioning life, but she simply refused to do anything without Blake. And Blake did not want to stop. According to Mitch, before the helicopter ride to Osea Island, Blake took him aside and said, 'I am going to Osea Island for Amy's sake. I have no intention of getting clean, I like being a drug addict.'

Staff told them they couldn't room together or see counsellors together, but Amy refused to engage with any treatment without her husband. This went against all medical advice. The upshot was that, even when Amy confessed, 'I don't mind it here', Blake was able to laugh and encourage her to leave. Which they did, after three days. A frantic crisis meeting between the doctors, the Winehouses, the label and Amy's management ensued, and they managed to get the couple back to Osea Island for a second stint two days later. Everyone was relieved, thinking they were at least cut off from a supply of drugs there. Who knows how, but someone managed to find a way onto the island, past security and into Blake and Amy's room. The newlyweds stayed just two days before leaving.

Rather than go home, Amy and Blake decamped to the Sanderson Hotel in Fitzrovia, a swanky part of central London. There, a succession of rows took place: first between Amy and her brother Alex, who was desperate with worry. Then between Amy and Blake: 'Bloodied and bruised Amy Winehouse stands by husband' ran the headline in the *Daily Mail* the next morning. Guests at the Sanderson had been alarmed by shouting, screaming and the clattering of furniture at 3 am that morning, and the photos accompanying the story showed Amy covered in bruises, bandages up her forearms, a huge bloody gash in her knee and blood spattered on her pink silk ballet slippers. Blake's face and neck were covered in thin scratches. Amy's face was smeared with eyeliner, mascara and tear tracks. Celebrity blogger Perez Hilton texted Amy to find out what had happened, and according to the *Daily Mail*, she had replied, 'Blake is the best man in the world. We would never ever harm each other ... I was cutting myself after he found me in our room about to do drugs with a call girl and rightly said I wasn't good enough for him. I lost it and he saved my life.'

After seeing the horrific pictures of his daughter, Mitch checked into a room in the Sanderson, hoping to keep an eye on the couple. But the next day they casually dropped into conversation that they'd decided to go on holiday to St Lucia in the Caribbean. While they were away, Amy's name was never far from the front pages.

Both the Civils and Mitch Winehouse were in and out of the press, accusing and defending each of their children alternately; and in early September the *News of the World* ran pictures of Amy with what appeared to be track marks on her arm. In the space of just nine months, Amy had gone from apparent good health and good habits to a frail, increasingly alienated junkie. She hadn't eaten well at the best of times, but now that she was on drugs her house was stuffed with Haribo packets and not much else. Her skin was constantly breaking out, her eyes had circles under them, and her teeth were coming loose. She'd leave the house with her make-up smeared down her face and her beehive falling off. Everything in Amy's world seemed as precariously balanced as that wig – and everyone seemed to be waiting for the day it tipped over into tragedy.

It was harder for friends and family to see and talk to Amy during this period of hotel living; Mitch and Janis both talk about Blake 'hovering' over her while she was on the phone to them, prompting her with questions about money. Tyler James, Amy's friend from Sylvia Young, said that although they'd always spoken regularly, Amy was phoning him three or four times a day during this period, abruptly hanging up mid-conversation when, Tyler assumed, Blake came back into the room. On the day of her twenty-fourth birthday, 14 September 2007, he arrived at her hotel room to take her to a party the family had planned. She answered the door with a bloody lip and tears running down her face, refusing to say what had happened. On her European tour that autumn, she and Blake were arrested and held overnight in Norway for marijuana possession.

The tone of press coverage changed: it was almost as if the papers were *willing* worse and worse things to happen. The way that Amy Winehouse was treated during this time was nothing short of abhorrent. Stories would run based on the flimsiest of sources about anything negative in her life. One day the Winehouses were horrified to read a story about Amy supposedly 'dying' in Blake's arms; as far as they knew, that had never happened. Comedians used Amy as the butt of their jokes, and paparazzi hounded her wherever she went. Her addictions became a punchline, her troubles a scary story used to warn others off. The situation really wasn't helped by her dad constantly agreeing to interviews to fight her corner and, some people suspected, further his own agenda. Amy was sanguine about inaccurate press reports. When Mitch was ranting about one paper publishing that she'd had an adrenaline shot when she collapsed in August, she just laughed and said, 'Yeah Dad, why let the truth get in the way of a good story?'

There were high points among the murk: that year she won a MOBO for Best UK Female, an MTV Award, made plans to go back to Miami to work with Salaam Remi again, and *Back to Black* was still selling well. But things were about to get worse.

The big plan was to launch Amy in America, where *Back to Black* was already enjoying moderate success. Some gigs were booked and then cancelled – Amy was gutted after failing a drug test, which meant she was denied a US visa. She seemed to finally appreciate the consequences of her drug use in a way that the medical warnings and pleas of her friends and family hadn't driven home. At the Hawley Arms with Mitch after she received the news, she rested her head against him and said, 'I want to clean up my act, Dad.'

The next day, police raided Amy and Blake's Camden flat, looking for Blake. He was due in court in November 2007 to face charges of GBH after he and a friend named Michael Brown had allegedly beaten the owner of the Macbeth pub for throwing Brown out. The victim, James King, had needed 12 hours of surgery after the assault. But the police were after Blake now for perverting the course of justice; he had tried to bribe King into not testifying. When the cops finally tracked him down to the flat where the couple were then living – in Bow, east London – they took Blake away in handcuffs, Amy hammering on the car window shouting, 'I'll be fine, I love you.'

When Blake was denied bail, Amy was as distraught as the people around her were relieved. He was sent to Pentonville Prison pending trial: perhaps with him out of the picture for a while, Amy would be more receptive to help? Perhaps she could spend more time with her family and friends; perhaps she would start writing songs again. All the horrors of the past six months suddenly seemed like they might be at an end. Hope reared its head again when, a few days later, Amy admitted she'd been to see a doctor who'd put her on Subutex – a drug-replacement treatment that was intended to wean her off heroin. Amy actually seeking out help herself was an excellent sign. Could this be the beginning of her recovery?

6

'This Is So Boring Without Drugs'

It had been a long, tough year, and as it drew to a close – with Blake in prison and Amy taking the first tentative steps towards recovery – Amy's team decided the best thing for her was to keep (or, in a sense, start) working. It had always been part of the plan for Raye, Amy's manager, at least. He felt that if she could be kept focused on music, then she would be more likely to stay away from her more damaging behaviours, and to feel better about herself. It had been his idea for Amy to go to the US; if she hadn't failed the drug test for her visa, this might also have been a turning point.

A UK tour had been planned for November 2007. Raye had been keen to populate the bus with Amy's friends and Mitch. The day before the whole circus set off on the road, Amy went to Pentonville to visit Blake for the first time. She found this experience more upsetting than the court appearances and the arrest itself; she barely slept that night, and her face was puffy and red, indicating hours of crying. The crew braced themselves for an eleventh-hour cancellation, but it never came. She got on the bus and off they went to Birmingham.

The journey went fairly smoothly. Amy seemed in reasonably good spirits with her friends around her, and although she talked about Blake almost constantly, she seemed completely sober as they pulled into the arena to unload. In the dressing room before the show she was nervous about going out on stage – the crowd was set to be about 15,000 people, and she still suffered from the stage fright of her younger years – but even half an hour before the show she seemed lucid, sober, on it.

Camera phones were not amazing in 2007, but even through their grainy eyes and the shaky fan-captured footage of that night, you can tell that Amy is drunk. She stumbles around the stage, seemingly disinterested in singing her own songs. Just as on *The Charlotte Church Show*, she struggles to find and keep to the beat and melody; as a jazz singer she had always improvised and noodled around during performances, but this wasn't a controlled showcase of vocal mastery: this was … well, it was quite bad. Shortly into the set, the crowd started booing. But Amy was feeling belligerent and sorry for herself, and jeered back, 'First of all, if you're booing, you're a mug for buying a ticket. Second, to all those booing: just wait till my husband gets out of incarceration. And I mean that.'

Amy couldn't get Blake off her mind. She started inserting his name into her songs and talking about him as if he was off fighting a righteous war rather than in prison awaiting trial for perverting the course of justice. At the side of the stage, Raye was worried. By this time he'd seen Amy at her best and her worst, and this was by far the worst live show she'd ever put on. Her erratic behaviour didn't stop when she left the stage, either: back in the dressing room she was tearful and exuberant by turns, at one point giving a friend's mum £20,000 for no obvious reason other than that she was drunk. When the crowds cleared out, leaving just Amy and Mitch alone, she turned back into that small child desperate for his approval. She was crying and apologizing, and rhapsodizing about how lucky she was to have her family around her. There was nothing that Mitch could say: he just held her and wondered what to do next.

Everyone agreed that there were some songs that were simply too hard for Amy to bear singing while Blake was locked up. So the tour continued without 'Wake Up Alone', 'Some Unholy War' and 'Back to Black'. This seemed to help for the next few shows, after which Amy told Raye she was serious about getting clean. She even said she would go to a clinic when the tour ended, and was open to whatever help they could work out for the remainder of the live dates. It was like the shows that had gone well had reminded her of what there was in life beyond Blake, beyond drink and beyond drugs. Like a cloud had been lifted. It didn't last long: two days later she was back in London, back on something and back to her old ways. This was the start of a period when Amy was impossible to predict: the bad days were scattered with good ones, which was almost worse than if she'd been consistently messed up. The good days kept raising everyone's hopes that the worst was behind her; but it never was.

Eventually, after a London show that was somewhere closer to the shambolic end of the Amy Winehouse scale, she asked to cancel the rest of the tour. Again, Mitch and

Raye pressed her on the subject of going to rehab, but she had a mental block about the subject; she just could not believe that it would help her. After all, she hadn't thrived in any other institutions – school and office work had simply felt like traps – so how would a medical institution be any different? 'I want to get better but I ain't doing rehab', was her response. Over the next few weeks, they trod water trying to figure out a way to help her without rehab as an option. Mitch describes her as stuck in a vicious circle: 'When Amy wasn't high, she wanted to get clean. Then she would get high and forget she wanted to get clean.'

To make matters worse, Amy had started hanging out with another bad influence: Pete Doherty was constantly round at her flat in Bow and, knowing his association with drugs, this was a development that Amy's friends didn't exactly welcome. The media hadn't backed off either, with paparazzi still constantly camped outside and stories about her appearing every couple of days – Amy Winehouse pictured running down the street in just a bra and jeans, Amy Winehouse hanging out with Pete Doherty, Amy Winehouse buying a pint of milk … Even Janis ended up embroiled in the press when a journalist tracked her down through her synagogue. She'd steered clear of giving interviews or stepping into the limelight, while Mitch had fully embraced it. Exhausted with worry and unable to see a way to get through to her daughter, this journalist managed to get her at a moment when she would just about try anything. 'It could just be the one thing that turns her around', he told her. The *News of the World* sent two journalists to her house to talk about Amy's brushes with death and framed it as an 'open letter' from Janis to her daughter, sneaking in family photos without her direct consent. 'I want you back. We want to help you, but we know that unless you want to be helped – unless you come to us – anything we tried would be in vain. So this letter is my way of making sure that you know that and we will do everything in our power to get you well again. After all, you are still my baby, and you always will be.' She asked for her fee to be donated to the MS Society.

Whether Amy saw the open letter or not, we don't know. She had other things to be worried about: she was being named as an official suspect in Blake's criminal case. The police suspected that Amy had provided the £200,000 Blake had tried to bribe James King with. Arrangements were made for her to meet with police at Shoreditch Police Station, where she had to be arrested before she was questioned; Raye went with her and ended up getting arrested himself when he got into a fight with some of the paparazzi outside. A sorry pair, but neither seemed in major trouble after that visit: Amy was released on bail without restrictions, and the charges against Raye were dropped.

At the end of the year, just as everything seemed in danger of slipping into a relentless mire, Amy had some good news. She'd been nominated for six Grammys and asked to perform at the ceremony in February 2008, in Los Angeles. She was thrilled in a way no one had seen for at least a year. She wanted to make the trip more than anything; but it would be dependent on her getting a visa, and for that she needed to be clean. 'Do you know what, Dad?', Amy said quietly on the phone as they discussed the nominations. 'This is just the beginning. I need to start writing again.'

Amy's oldest friends hadn't seen much of her in the previous few months. Ever since the disastrous weeks after Amy's seizure, they'd found it hard to speak to their old friend who seemed hellbent on destroying her life. They had lobbied long and hard for Amy's family to force her into residential rehab; when that hadn't happened, they'd kept their distance. But now Amy really wanted them around her, planning a holiday with them and Tyler for the end of December 2007.

While she was away, Amy ended up staying with Bryan Adams in the West Indies, on the private island of Mustique. The two had met in London and evidently hit it off, although who knows how much he regretted extending the invite when she went into withdrawal. Raye managed to talk her out of leaving the island because he was convinced that she wanted to track down some drugs, and Bryan Adams became worried about her weight as the process of withdrawal led to constant vomiting. When she said she wanted to come back to London 'to show Blake she was off heroin', no one believed her – rehabilitation takes longer than a few days, and in London she would have much easier access to drugs again. But she couldn't be dissuaded and came back to the UK after just a week away.

Amy's personal troubles hadn't stopped her being in high demand though, and on her return, Raye told her that the makers of the next James Bond film, *Quantum of Solace*, wanted her to write and sing the title song. This is a big deal for any singer and Amy was excited, immediately calling Mark Ronson to ask him to work with her on it. The timing couldn't have been better as far as her team were concerned – if Amy wanted to perform at the Grammys she'd need to pass a drugs test on 22 January; this meant that after 15 January, no drugs could enter her system, even the Valium she was now being prescribed to help her relax. Amy loved working with Mark, and Raye and the rest of her team hoped that focusing on the Bond theme would keep her mind off the hunt for drugs.

Amy worked hard to be completely clean in the run-up to that crucial, drug-free week. She was constantly on edge; it felt like a race against time. No one was really sure if she could make it. Even she wasn't sure. Every minute dragged by like it was a year long. Right before the test week, it almost seemed as if she was going to be able to do it. She was steering clear of drugs and laughing and joking like the old Amy, lulling everyone into a false sense of security, as she had done so many times before. Then, on 14 January, Tyler James called Mitch with bad news: Amy had used. It was no use now – the test was scheduled and what would be would be.

But then, another curveball. On the day of the test, the *Sun* published photos of Amy supposedly taking crack cocaine. It turned out that two of Blake's friends had secretly filmed her in order to sell the footage to the papers. Again, Amy was sanguine about the whole fiasco: 'What do I care? Everybody thinks I take drugs anyway.' As a result, the drug test was postponed for a week, and a planned concert in Cannes was cancelled. In fact, all future plans were cancelled: her record label finally put their foot down. She was not going to be allowed to perform at all until she went to rehab. No Grammys, no BRITS, no nothing. After a big, tense meeting with her team at Island and her two doctors, Amy finally agreed to try rehab. Although she desperately tried to take it back in Mitch's cab on the way there, she was admitted to the private psychiatric Capio Nightingale Hospital in London's St John's Wood.

Amy seemed to settle into the Capio Nightingale. The first few days involved a lot of sleeping and rest, and eventually she began eating and feeling slightly better. She also talked about moving out of the flat in Bow, where a lot of the people who enabled her addiction were constantly found. This indicated that she was serious about getting clean. Her withdrawal and drug-substitute medication once again led to constant vomiting, and after some days of this she was transferred to a private clinic in central London for rehydration. While she was there, she decided she wanted to go home – she was feeling better, she said, and didn't see the point in going back to the Capio Nightingale. She was okay now! She was done! This time everyone was firm with her: she had to go back. But, as she hadn't been sectioned (under the UK Mental Health Act; committed), she could technically leave whenever she felt like it.

The delayed Grammys drug test took place during this period, at a time when Amy was looking and feeling almost back to her old self. But a few days later, a drug dealer who had been around Blake and Amy from the start of Amy's addictions smuggled drugs into the Capio Nightingale, stuffed in a teddy bear. Although a close, trusted friend had been visiting at the time, Amy still managed to take some before he got rid of the remainder. It was another frustrating setback that made all her progress seem like a mirage. To add to that, her US visa didn't come through – traces of cocaine had been found in her blood. Amy sobbed when she found out that she couldn't travel to perform at the ceremony in person, but Raye had a back-up plan: a live video-link between the event in LA and Amy in Hammersmith, playing an intimate show to family and friends.

The events of those days proved the final straw for Amy and she put her foot down: she wouldn't return to the Capio Nightingale. Neither her team, nor her doctors, nor her family were happy about it, but they struck a deal with her: she could move out to a hotel with her clean friend (a photographer known to the family as 'American Blake' – he was American, and also named Blake) and take regular drug tests. If she tested positive, the Grammys link-up would be pulled. She agreed. The show went ahead.

Riverside Studios was decked out in opulent reds and blacks for the show, the vast studio given the look and feel of an intimate club. It was filled with round dining tables that seated invited guests. Amy performed a private show before the Grammys link-up went live at 11.30 pm. She was flawless – if you'd been living under a rock for the past year, you'd never have guessed that this woman had been to hell and back, and was still struggling through recovery. For the ceremony in LA, she played 'You Know I'm No Good' and 'Rehab', which could have felt grimly ironic. But the cheers from both crowds were a welcome distraction; she had smashed it. She also won five of the six Grammys she was nominated for: Record of the Year, Song of the Year, Best New Artist, Best Pop Vocal Album and Best Female Pop Vocal Performance. The icing on the cake came when her idol, jazz singer Tony Bennett, presented Record of the Year. 'I can't believe it', she said. 'Tony Bennett knows my name.' She dedicated her awards to her mum and dad, who both rushed the stage to hug her. She was drug-free and adored.

The party continued into the night after Amy's section of the show was over; she seemed to be having a good time, but at one point beckoned her old friend Juliette backstage for a quiet minute away from the madness. She'd been dancing and grinning for hours, seeming happy and healthy and at the top of her game. But what she said next simply shattered her friend: 'Jules, this is so boring without drugs.'

The earth-shattering truth of that statement was driven home when Amy managed to circumvent all the security processes that had been put in place at her hotel and have drugs delivered; she was still addicted and nowhere near out of the woods. It seemed particularly crushing after the euphoria of Grammys night, another cruel corkscrew in the great rollercoaster of recovery. Unfortunately, things escalated and it wasn't long before Amy was back at home, regularly getting high and refusing to engage with treatment of any kind. During this period she cancelled obligations, missed visits to see Blake (although phone calls remained constant) and just kept on using.

Abruptly, in March 2008, she moved house. Although the new flat was just around the corner from Jeffrey's Place, she announced that it was a fresh start. She wanted to get clean, and she wanted to do it quickly. It was great news but tempered once again by the fact that she refused to go to a residential rehab. 'I want to do the detox and withdrawal here', she told Mitch, who relented almost immediately, arranging for her doctors to come over and discuss the process. Two nurses were hired to stay with her and administer the drug-replacement medication. On day one, the whole thing was thrown off course because Amy had taken heroin. They tried again, but the same thing happened. It seemed hopeless, even as she tried to start work on the Bond theme she'd been asked to write. One day she'd be sleeping, withdrawing or chattering in a rambling way about anything because she was high on crack; the next she'd have a productive day and offer glimpses of her old self. But these were always followed by another bad day, days when Amy was self-harming, punching mirrors and stubbing cigarettes out on her cheek, crying and screaming hysterically. The vicious cycle was back in full effect.

'I'm all right, Mum, I really am', was how Amy greeted Janis after the worst of these episodes, 'but I want to give up drugs.' She kept repeating it like a mantra, pale, thin, barefoot on the gravel pathway outside the studio she'd been working in. Family members from this time describe Amy as not entirely whole; her stepbrother Michael (Janis's partner's son) described her as 'empty', and Janis felt there was 'a part of her that was not really with it at all'. It was as though the part of Amy that made her Amy had been locked up, and only the shell remained. Even when she won her second Ivor for 'Love Is a Losing Game', she turned up too late to collect the award and was distracted all night. Pink Floyd's David Gilmore accepted his lifetime achievement award by saying, 'Let's hope in about another 20 or 30 years, Amy Winehouse will get one of these long-service gongs.' It was a good day, Amy was lucid and at least bodily present. Everyone laughed; a room full of people ready to believe she could make it through this.

7

'Dad, I'm Not That Stupid'

Even if it hadn't been exploitative and judgemental in tone, the relentless press coverage around this time was almost pointless. In his 2015 documentary *Amy*, Asif Kapadia shows clips from media outlets around the world, the bullying she received from every corner of the media. 'That section could have been 25 minutes long', he said at the time. 'Longer, even. There's stuff from Brazil. There's stuff from America. There's stuff from everywhere. So much of it is negative. It's industrial international bullying. It's open season. And she can't fire back. People say all publicity is good publicity. But that's a lie. More and more you see people laughing at her online and sharing clips on YouTube.' It wasn't even telling anyone anything they hadn't already seen the day before: Amy's a mess, Amy's still a mess, Amy continues to be a mess … the story glitched now and then when, say, Blake's trial took place and he pleaded guilty to GBH and conspiracy to pervert the course of justice, but the narrative the tabloids were peddling didn't really go anywhere new. If anything, it began to irritate readers. Why can't she just sort herself out? It's been going on for so long, it's her own fault. Why do I hear about it all the time? There was very little attempt to explain or understand the nature of addiction and people began to feel that their empathy reserves had been used up.

Meanwhile, Amy's health was worsening. After a whistle-stop trip to Russia to play Roman Abramovich's private party (as you do), Amy was at home with some friends when she went pale and her eyes rolled back in her head as her body started to convulse. A friend caught her before she hit the ground, and she was rushed to the London Clinic on Harley Street, where she'd previously been for rehydration during detox. The test results were not good. This was the most shocking prognosis Amy had received to date and it did seem to sink in a little: she had mucus all around her lungs, which was causing her to cough and wheeze; her voice was damaged and it was possible that she had nodules on her vocal cords; a growth had appeared in her chest cavity that wasn't cancerous but needed keeping an eye on; and years of smoking cigarettes and, later, crack had brought on the early stages of emphysema. Whether it was the danger of losing her voice or the danger of losing her life, this news seemed to hit Amy harder than previous diagnoses. Never one to be left speechless, she went very quiet as the doctors kept talking, listing more and more of the problems her tiny body was facing. Later, after sitting quietly in her room at the clinic for a while, she asked for nicotine patches and stuck them all over.

Amy was in a strange emotional state at this point in her life. It was as though reality no longer existed to her; she was in and out of the London Clinic, waiting for news of Blake's sentencing, not working, not writing, not doing much of anything as the summer drew on. She was floating through a kind of suspended animation. She couldn't look much beyond her own life. Context was almost entirely lost on her – take, for example, when she met Nelson Mandela. A huge, historic concert was being put on in Hyde Park to celebrate his ninetieth birthday, and he was being honoured with performances by the likes of Razorlight, Will Smith and Josh Groban. Amy was set to perform and was introduced to Mandela backstage as then Prime Minister Gordon Brown gave him a tour. According to Brown, Amy shook hands with Nelson Mandela and said, 'Mr Mandela, my husband and you have a great deal in common. You've both spent a long time in prison.' Quite what Nelson Mandela made of this comparison we will never know – we can only hope he had no idea who Blake Fielder-Civil was. But plenty of people were rankled by Amy switching up the words to 'Free Nelson Mandela' to sing instead, 'Free Blakey, my fella.' When a buzzing Amy proudly told her about this a few days later, Janis rolled her eyes. She later analyzed Amy's actions, writing, 'Her emotions and everything going on in her world continued to consume her to the point where I think she was oblivious to the occasion.'

This period of semi-recovery came abruptly to an end in July 2008 when Blake was sentenced to 27 months in prison. Amy took it hard – harder than the original arrest. She was consumed by a kind of grief, unable to leave the house and sleeping almost constantly. She seemed to want to function and simply couldn't: one day she was on her way to the gym but got to her front door and just could not open it. Her bedroom had become her sanctuary, just as it had when she was a child. The only people who really saw much of Amy during this time were her newly employed security staff, led by Andrew Morris. With them basically living with her, it was almost impossible for Amy to have drugs delivered (although she tried any number of inventive ways), and they shielded the family from her when she was at her worst. Photographers were still camped outside her front door 24 hours a day; they were becoming more than a nuisance. On 28 July, Mitch was visiting Amy when she started coughing and struggling desperately for breath; she was in the midst of another seizure. An ambulance was called but the paparazzi made it difficult to pull up in front of the house. In the end, Amy was rushed out covered by a blanket.

After these setbacks, Amy started rebelling against the doctors' advice again. She'd always had trouble taking orders and respecting any kind of authority figure that wasn't Cynthia, and the doctors became another set of boring figureheads stopping her from doing what she wanted. Between them, the label and Amy's management decided to cancel her remaining gigs that summer – Amy had wanted to do them, but it was clear after a particularly shaky performance at the V Festival that she was too fragile to do so. It was impossible to disguise her trembling hands and damaged voice, but more than that, there was something about her that had gone missing; a light in her eyes that was dulled. It was as though Amy had completely lost confidence both onstage and off. She was so nervous to meet her brother's new girlfriend, Riva, that she behaved like a timid kitten, listening in to the conversation from her mezzanine above the living room, occasionally interjecting comments but scurrying back out of sight any time that Riva looked up.

Just as there had been for years, there were the occasional signs that Amy was emerging from the deep jungle of her addictions; she periodically checked herself into the London Clinic, she seemed to be putting on a bit of weight and her security team seemed effective in stemming the flow of drugs into her home. Amy even surprised Janis with a new home to help her extricate herself from a relationship; Janis hadn't realized Amy was even aware of what was going on in her life at that point. Amy even donated two of her cats (Moggy and Minty) to the new bungalow. Ever since she'd moved out of her mum's house, Amy had collected cats. At one point she had 16, which was quite a pungent situation; it wasn't pleasant or unusual to stumble across cat poo in the most unlikely of nooks and crannies.

Although Amy still refused any kind of psychological help, the setbacks became fewer and further between. Mitch in particular was still concerned about the hold Blake had over his daughter and the two rowed about it regularly, but the general feeling was that if they could keep Amy away from her husband, it might just give her the time and space to get clean. According to Mitch, Blake had called him to say he wanted a divorce, which Mitch saw as more mind games from the Fielder-Civil camp, as Blake certainly hadn't mentioned divorce to his wife. A letter from him to Amy talked about them being Bonnie and Clyde, that they were destined to be together forever; the next day he'd spoken to Mitch and said he'd start divorce proceedings if Mitch helped him financially. Amy was keen to support Blake's recovery; she still saw a future with him, but it seemed that Blake wasn't on the same page.

Never one to stay out of the papers for long, Blake soon agreed to an interview with the *News of the World*. He told the paper, 'I dragged Amy into drugs and without me there is no doubt that she would never have gone down that road. I ruined something beautiful ... I will do anything for her, and that includes walking away. If Amy wants a divorce, I'm not going to fight her for anything. It's going to be the saddest day of my life.' The article threw Amy into a rage, convinced that he'd been manipulated or misquoted by the journalist – but then Mitch showed her a text message Blake had sent him that day. It read, 'You are trying to buy your daughter's divorce. Stop hiding Amy's money. I want a contract.' She was taken aback by what she read. For what might have been the second time in her life, she was at a loss for words. We can only imagine what was running through her mind, what papered-over cracks in her heart were opening back up. Mitch remembers the conversation clearly because it made so little sense to him. 'I love him, Dad. I'll love him no matter what', she said quietly. 'I'm stronger now, and what he says to you only makes me want to get clean and stay clean. Then I can help him get clean as well.'

When Blake escaped his prison-sanctioned rehab (that Amy paid for) to visit her at the London Clinic, he arrived with drugs. After a brief visit, Blake handed himself back in to the police and Amy retrieved the drugs from under her pillow. 'Dad, I'm not that stupid', she said as she handed them over. She took Blake's visit and return to prison in her stride rather than falling apart as she may have done just weeks earlier. It felt as though Blake's hold over her had lessened slightly; at the very least, the drugs' had.

Just before Christmas, Amy decided she wanted to go back to St Lucia. She was still on a drug replacement named Subutex and continued taking it while she was away. It was a long stint in the Caribbean and Janis flew out to surprise her in February, but it was Janis who got the real surprise: Amy looked tanned, had put on weight and seemed happy for the first time in months. The tabloids all had photographers trying to follow her around and stories had appeared in the press claiming she'd been crawling around island bars begging for drinks, but it didn't seem that way to Janis. Amy seemed more together than she had for months.

Just a couple of days after her mum arrived, though, Amy abruptly decided to go back to the UK. There was no explanation, no guilty feelings for disappearing just as her visitor had arrived – classic Amy. She and Janis said an emotional goodbye on the beach, and Janis was just sadly settling back into her seat when she looked up and there on the horizon was Amy, astride a huge black horse. It was like something out of a film, a little sprinkling of magic that suggested maybe she did feel bad for leaving after all.

The reason for her sudden departure became clear later; she'd found out that Blake was out of prison and back in rehab in Sheffield. There are reports of Amy visiting Sheffield and speaking with Blake regularly, but she wasn't the only woman he'd been in touch with. Then in early March, Amy faced a new wave of controversy: the year before she'd attended a Prince's Trust fundraiser, and in the crush of photographers, security people and fans around her, a fan had been hit in the face. On 5 March, Amy was charged with assault and released on bail without conditions. (Eventually she was acquitted after a court case in which she kicked her shoes off and waggled her feet in front of the judge, saying, 'Could someone with feet this small be intimidating?'.) Life back in London was harder than life in St Lucia. In St Lucia she'd been happy, but in London everything was a hassle, and she'd had enough. So she went back.

Janis visited her again that May and found a very different Amy to the last time. She was back down to a size six, picking only at junk food she sent people to get her from the other side of the island. She was 24 but could fit into children's clothes; something wasn't right. Amy's issues with food were becoming clearer without the complication of the drugs, but as with her drinking, everyone was focused on kicking the drugs first. The other issues? They could wait.

Amy had agreed (reluctantly) to play the St Lucia Jazz Festival. It began portentously with dark storm clouds gathering. As show time got closer, the humidity built and became almost unbearable; the wind that was gradually whipping up was almost a relief, but it did nothing to lessen the tension in the air. The storm broke shortly before Amy's set, and rain was hammering down by the time she came on, walking out gingerly in heels that she took off, then put on again, then took off again as the show wore on. She was constantly clutching the hem of her dress like it was a security blanket. The show was not going well: she was nervous, and she was drunk. After less than an hour, she stumbled off stage. 'What happened last night, Amy?', Janis asked the next evening, when Amy finally emerged from her room. Her reaction was very different to the way she'd laughed off the disastrous *Charlotte Church Show* performance years before. 'Don't, Mum', she said. 'I'm too embarrassed.'

Amy stayed in the Caribbean for some weeks more, during which time her drinking seemed to take over. The old bully in her resurfaced and she had constant arguments with friends. She'd emerge late in the day hungover and demand shots; when her companions tried to tell her it was a bad idea, she'd rage and demand doubles. The drugs seemed to be out of her system – 'I'm not going back to drugs, Mum', she told Janis when she finally returned to the UK. 'I'm bored with it'. But their absence was throwing into sharp relief just how serious her other problems were.

When she finally returned from St Lucia, Amy moved to a house in Hadley Wood, a leafy suburb just outside London. Away from Camden, where she still had a flat, she was at less risk of relapsing but at much higher risk of boredom. She rattled around in a huge house that Mitch had rented for her, all fancy columns and palm trees out front. It never quite felt like home, despite the fact that her cat collection grew (Monkey, Melina, Chops, Kodger, Rita, Shirley, Garry and Kola-Bottle were joined by seemingly new feline faces every day) and her Elvis Presley phone rang constantly. He'd swing his hips and sing 'Hound Dog' whenever a call came in, echoing into the hallway. She had a cleaner who came twice a week, but with Amy's natural messiness, tendency to throw parties and countless cats in residence, the place was a constant pigsty. Although it was outside London, Hadley Wood was within fairly easy reach of the north London boroughs where Janis and Alex lived. They'd pop over to see her at least once a week, but you could never really predict what you'd find when you popped over to see Amy. Sometimes she refused to come downstairs or couldn't be woken; other times she'd be full of beans. She had a tendency to receive people enthusiastically one minute and disappear the next, not to be seen again for the rest of the day. On one visit, Janis and her new partner Richard overheard Amy on the phone. Through the tinny phone speakers they heard Blake's reedy voice. 'I can't talk to you when you're drunk. I can't meet you when you're like this – you hit and punch me when you're drunk.' They were still in touch, despite the fact that in July that year their divorce had been finalized, but it seemed that even Blake was struggling to deal with Amy and her alcoholism.

Amid the worrying lows, the inevitable high point rolled around and brought Salaam Remi with it. Her old producer had come to visit, with a view to getting Amy back to work. His calm demeanour seemed to cool her hot temper, and she worked intently with him for several days. Occasionally she would check into the London Clinic, but since there was no psychological element to her treatment, she'd begun using it a bit like a hotel. Drying out for a few days, then ordering room service and making a nuisance of herself before returning home. She wasn't deathly thin at this point, but she still worried about her body. Although she'd had a full figure as a teenager, the years of drugs and eating disorders that had ravaged her figure had left her with a much smaller chest. She became self-conscious about it, wearing two padded bras at a time to try to give the illusion of larger breasts. One day she casually announced that she was going to have breast implants, as if she'd been flicking through a catalogue and seen something she wanted.

Her drinking continued to wreak havoc on her friends and family. The cycle was like a more drawn-out version of when she was on drugs: she'd spend a few weeks constantly drunk and then spend a few weeks completely sober. Amy decided to host a birthday party for her brother and spent all night drunkenly screeching at anyone who tried to go near the jukebox. At the Q Awards that year she turned up late, heckled Robert Plant and interrupted the Specials' acceptance speech. In December 2009, she went to a pantomime performance of *Cinderella* in Milton Keynes – a strange thing to do at the best of times, but not necessarily something we can blame on alcohol. During the performance she was clearly intoxicated, that huge voice booming out, 'He's fucking behind you!' She got even less PG as the show went on, calling out, 'Fuck Cinders, Prince Charming marry me' and calling the Ugly Sisters 'bitches'. When front-of-house manager Richard Pound intervened, she punched him, pulled his hair and kicked him in a very sensitive area. She was arrested the next day for common assault and disorder, pleaded guilty and was given a two-year conditional discharge and ordered to pay costs.

Clearly, Amy still needed help. Her doctors started her on a new drug to help calm her anxiety and ease alcohol withdrawal, and she was still in and out of the clinic, despite her disruptive behaviour when she was there. Still she resisted any attempts to talk about the underlying mental health issues. 'I have everything I've ever wanted', Amy told Naomi, her stylist and friend. 'I shouldn't be feeling like this, but

I am.' The following year began in much the same way: a week here or there in the London Clinic, and a trip to Jamaica to record a track for Quincy Jones's seventy-fifth birthday album. During all this time, she was still seeing Blake and even talked about remarrying him. But then something happened that put Blake out of her mind for good. Amy Winehouse fell in love with someone new.

Reg Traviss was tall, handsome and just Amy's type. She first spotted him at his parents' pub and asked him out for a drink; she was smitten. She started talking about settling down, marrying Reg and having kids. Who knows if that was just the blush of new love talking, but Amy had often told interviewers how she saw herself in ten years: settled, a mother, happy. Reg was a film director and his schedule was erratic; sometimes they wouldn't see each other until he turned up at her door at 4 am, shattered from a night shoot. Sometimes he'd just head home to sleep.

Amy was keeping wild hours too, sleeping in late and drinking until the wee hours. She was in another cycle of heavy drinking when she was meant to be heading to Europe for a brief tour. The first night was in Serbia, in the capital city of Belgrade. The crowd was restless; once again, Amy was running late. When she finally ambled out to the microphone, she could barely stand. Her band would strike up a rhythm and she'd start singing, only to stop and wander over to one of them to whisper in his ear. She took her shoes off, she put them back on again. She grinned glassy-eyed into the crowd, like a naughty toddler. She sat down. She barely sang. The crowd was disgruntled and there were 'boos' that grew louder as the set wore on. It seemed obvious that this show should have been cancelled; according to Asif Kapadia's 2015 documentary, *Amy*, she had wanted to cancel and someone had put her on the plane while she was passed out. Either way, it put paid to the rest of the tour.

Back in London, Amy spent her days at home watching YouTube videos of her past performances and digging out old photos. She was back in the cycle of staying sober for some weeks then relenting and hitting the bottle again. Her doctor, Cristina Romete, was very worried. She typed up a letter outlining her very real fears for Amy; if something didn't change, Amy would die.

8

'Is She Dead?'

Amy Winehouse was a terrible drummer. Everyone in her life knew it, and told her, but it didn't stop her having a good old try. She'd bash away at the drumkit at all hours in her apartment in Camden Square, where she'd moved after leaving the boredom of Hadley Wood behind. She didn't keep to a traditional circadian rhythm: she was awake when she was awake and asleep when she was asleep, 24-hour clock be damned. So after an hour of incessant bashing, like the sound of a whole kitchen's worth of pans falling down an elevator shaft, it was no wonder that Andrew poked his head round the door and asked her to maybe take a break. It was 2 am. It was 23 July 2011.

* * * * *

On 22 July, Mitch flew to New York to play some shows of his own. The day before he left, Amy called him and asked him to come over. She'd been digging around through her things and found some photographs from when she and Alex were little – everyone thought they'd been lost in one of the various moves around London, but here they were. Two chubby, dark-haired kids looking angelic, bringing various family memories back to life. 'You've *got* to come over,' she insisted.

The kitchen table was covered in photos and Amy picked them up one by one, laughing, reminiscing. There was one of Cynthia – 'Wasn't Nan beautiful?' – and pictures of Alex were met with pride and a bit of ribbing. They spent all afternoon going through the photos before Mitch had to leave; they parted with a promise to record a song together, when he got back from New York. They'd promised each other this many times before and it had never happened, but it had been a long time since Amy had brought it up. It felt good to hear her making plans, and when Mitch hugged her goodbye, he felt how much stronger her body was. As he pulled the cab out of the driveway, he turned and waved goodbye.

The next day, Janis and her husband Richard proposed visiting Amy for the first time since the disastrous Belgrade show and the cancellation of the European tour. It had been a bit of a wake-up call for Amy, and Andrew told them that she'd had a few dry weeks between then and now, but that this week had been a bad one. Although she'd been on good form with Mitch the day before, that hadn't lasted. They could come over if they wanted, but he wasn't sure what state Amy would be in. Janis was set: it was time to see her daughter. When they arrived just after lunch, they felt a tingle of fear: there were smashed wine bottles on the patio and a pained look in Andrew's eyes. Amy was asleep, but Janis was determined to wait until she emerged.

They settled round the kitchen table, still covered in the old photos Amy had found the day before. Janis picked through them, just as Mitch had – photos of Amy and

Alex as children, Janis and Mitch's wedding, and Amy's beloved Cynthia. It was as though Amy had been on a walk down memory lane, reliving happy family times. Janis felt mixed feelings as she and Richard sifted through them: the warmth of those days and her smiling, vibrant daughter made the cold quiet of the kitchen that day seem ominous. Andrew offered to try to wake Amy, then came down half an hour later with her over his shoulder in a fireman's lift. Janis looked at her daughter slumped over the table, barely coherent, barely awake. The sharp tang of alcohol rose from her even though Andrew had obviously tried to clean her up a bit before bringing her down. Janis had never known Amy to be so drunk she had to be carried. It was deeply upsetting. No one knew what to say as Amy slowly came round.

'You're looking at the photos, Mum.' Her voice was heavy, slurring words into one long, tortuous sludge. She picked up a photo of Alex as a baby and tried to focus on it. Janis still couldn't speak. 'Wasn't Alex a beautiful baby?', Amy slurred, before dropping the picture and slumping back onto the table, as if the string holding her head up had been cut. Janis and Richard sat with her in silence for another ten minutes, until it hurt too much to be there anymore. 'We're going to go now, Amy', Janis said gently. As Amy tried to stand, Janis pulled her up and wrapped her arms around her. Amy clung to her neck desperately as Janis whispered how worried she was, how she hated to see her like this.

'I'm sorry Mummy, I love you Mummy', Amy cried into her neck. 'I love you too', Janis said. And they left.

* * * * *

Earlier in the evening, pre-drumming, Amy had called Andrew over and said, 'Look at this.'

'She was showing me some clips on her laptop and she was singing and she said, "Boy, I can sing", and I said, "Damn right, you can sing"', he recalled. She was pensive. Quiet. 'She said, "If I could I would give it back just to walk down the street with no hassle, I would."'

After Andrew asked Amy to give the drums a rest, he went back downstairs. Shortly after that, he heard footsteps from Amy's room, the occasional peal of laughter and then the quiet that indicated she had fallen asleep. The house was silent, peaceful.

When he woke the next morning, Andrew went up to Amy's room and found her asleep, face smushed into the pillow. There were empty vodka bottles around the bed and the stale smell of vomit in the air. He left her to lie in until she was ready to get up.

Around 3.30 pm he decided to check on her again – alarm bells weren't ringing as she was a late riser at the best of times, so it was with no great sense of urgency that he climbed the stairs and gently knocked on the door to her room. When he opened it, though, something was off. The room felt … weird. After a second, he realized that Amy hadn't moved since he'd poked his head in that morning, not a muscle. He rushed over to the bed as the creeping fear consumed him: she wasn't breathing. She was gone.

* * * * *

The days that followed Amy's death were a blur for all the Winehouses. Mitch flew back overnight in a daze, reliving the phone call he'd received from Andrew the day before. 'Is she dead?', he'd asked for the second time in his life. The family gathered at Janis's house, where she sat, unable to process what was happening, relieved to have others around her to take over the admin. Alex had been desperate to see his sister, but Camden Square was a circus. News vans had set up shop and devastated fans lined the pavement. Because no one was yet sure how or why she'd died, the police were treating it as a crime scene: no one was allowed in. Stuck outside in the car, Alex and Richard had watched surreal scenes unfold, as they tend to do in the aftermath of a death. One of Amy's cats was bundled up and handed to a shell-shocked Reg, while fans left increasingly wild tributes outside, from huge hand-drawn portraits to packets of cigarettes and bottles of wine and vodka propped up amid the cards, notes and flowers.

It was a dry, grey day in north London on 26 July. A decoy funeral had been planned under the name 'Winehouse' elsewhere, while 'Emma Shaffer' was due to be celebrated in a ceremony at Edgwarebury Cemetery and cremated at Golders Green Crematorium in the same hall as her grandmother five years before. Like Cynthia, Amy hadn't wanted to be buried. The service was short, private and emotional: friends had washed and prepared Amy's body, dressing her in the iconic yellow dress she'd worn to the BRITs in 2007, while the Carole King song 'So Far Away' closed the service. Celebrities rubbed shoulders with Amy's family and school friends, leading to stories that would be funny if it hadn't been such a dark day, like Bryan Adams grabbing a lift between ceremonies with Richard's son and being coerced into a rendition of 'Love a Woman'.

Mitch was the only family member to speak at the service. He talked about Amy the star, Amy the singer and Amy the girl who'd scribbled her hopes and dreams into notebooks and painted her room like a Hokusai painting. The girl who loved cats and KFC and Haribo, and had a dancing Elvis Presley phone in her front hall. He ended the eulogy with a story about a school notebook of Amy's that Richard had recently found. It was from 1995, shortly after Janis and Mitch had divorced. Amy had drawn a heart split into segments, each representing the people she loved the most – Alex, her mum and her dad. 'She wrote that she missed me. I had never seen this before', Mitch told the congregation. 'In the last entry in the school book she wrote: "I love to live … and I live to love". She was just twelve years old. Goodnight my angel, sleep tight. Mummy and Daddy love you so much.'

Epilogue

A ny cursory search of YouTube with the words 'Amy Winehouse cover' will net you thousands of results. There are videos uploaded hours ago and videos uploaded more than a decade ago. There are girls with backcombed hair and eyeliner, and boys doing comedy skits. There are professional bands and people sitting alone in front of a webcam in their bedrooms. There are some with thousands of views and some with fewer than ten. It's been ten years since Amy Winehouse died but there is no sign of her music losing its potency.

If you walk through Camden Stables, you can visit a funny little statue of Amy. It seems impossible that it can be lifesized – a tiny, doll-like figure whose proportions don't seem real. The statue isn't great – it's not really somewhere that hardcore Amy fans would visit to remember her – but it attracts a steady trade of gingerly approaching tourists, wrapping friendship bands around those tiny bronze wrists, posing awkwardly for photos with her image. Amy doesn't really need a statue in Camden; she's everywhere already.

In fact, Amy influenced far more than hopeful young singers. She bridged the gap between generations with *Back to Black*, beloved by both young people and their parents; weaving traditional soul, jazz and nostalgic harmonies into a contemporary pop record wasn't something that anyone had really pulled off with aplomb in the 2000s, and

Back to Black's success really paved the way for a whole new wave of acts that mined the fifties and sixties. It's hard to imagine Amy's BRIT School classmate Adele reaching the sheer heights of success that she has without *Back to Black* coming before her; nor Paloma Faith's retro leanings being so easily received. Amy's success in America also increased (and prolonged) interest in Britain's women across the pond. It has been optimistically termed a second British Invasion – the first being The Beatles – but while that's debatable, Amy certainly helped to cement Adele and Emeli Sandé as stars in the US. Without her, would current acts like Ellie Goulding and Dua Lipa be enjoying success in America?

Refusing to act like a primped and proper pop princess was wildly refreshing in the staid 2000s pop scene. It's no wonder that Amy's brand of humour played out on irreverent shows like *Popworld* and *Never Mind the Buzzcocks*, which were built on snark and a refusal to take celebrity too seriously. More than that, Amy opened the door to female performers who perhaps didn't fit the chart-dictated norms. Lady Gaga's weirdness was more obvious than Amy's – Amy may not have gone for a dress made out of meat, even if it had shown off her boobs in a particularly lascivious way – but she was probably given more opportunities to lean into those oddities because Amy Winehouse had completely changed what it was to be a successful woman pop star. Media training was out; referencing cat AIDs and deriding Dido was in.

It's easy to forget just how few women musicians were considered 'credible' by the music industry and the wider public. The prevailing feeling was that women were puppets of a male writing and management team, 'manufactured' and manipulated by an industry behind them, rather than independent artists in their own rights. Amy smashed this misconception and strode through the music industry with as much forthright bluster as any identikit indie boy. Florence Welch, of Florence and the Machine, remembers seeing Amy at Glastonbury and thinking, 'Wow, there is a place for female singer-songwriters in this world.' Her deeply personal songwriting style also influenced singers who put a premium on 'authenticity', offering a blueprint for how to make the tiny details of your personal experience feel like something shared by everyone. Lana Del Rey, in particular, took this to heart and has acknowledged Amy's influence on the long career she has crafted out of doing something very similar.

'Amy paved the way for artists like me and made people excited about British music again', Adele wrote in a 2011 tribute. 'I don't think she ever realized just how brilliant she was and how important she is.'

* * * * *

It never fails to surprise me how often you can be walking around London – or any major city, really – and turn a corner to be faced, unexpectedly, with Amy's face. She's been the subject of exhibitions, graffiti artists – anyone who's struck by a strong look made up of bold shapes and colours. She feels like a universal figure; someone we all have our own memories of, songs that we've knit emotional attachments to. No matter your feelings on her personal life, there are very few musicians whose music has staked a claim on our collective attention in the same way.

You'd hope that the story of Amy Winehouse has also led to some changes in the way that artists are cared for by their labels and management teams. Although the buck ultimately stopped with Amy herself, when you see her story laid out in black and white it feels like there are pivotal moments where help could – and should – have been offered. Was she supported enough when she was constantly being hounded by paparazzi? Should the label have sat back and let her spend years doing little other than getting high and drunk with the cushion of work available whenever she felt like coming back to it? Could her family have cared for her differently? Of course, as I've said before, hindsight is 20/20 and addiction, eating disorders and mental illnesses are all incredibly difficult to diagnose, manage or treat without the person in question's willingness to address them. Amy wanted to treat her symptoms, but she never wanted anyone to get into the causes. It's ironic that, for a woman who wore her heart on her sleeve musically, she was terrified of anyone discovering the real her.

Times have changed since 2011. The rise of social media has been a double-edged sword, but you can argue that we have become much more empathetic and aware of issues that we've previously been blind to, or that exist slightly outside the norms that newspapers and television have dictated for decades. Gender and sexuality are much more openly discussed; mental health education is vastly better, and disorders are more openly addressed; the dangers of alcohol are more widely understood. The glamourization of drugs and alcohol has also lessened in the years since Amy's death. 'Heroin chic' and lad culture have both faced a severe backlash. On 14 September 2011, Amy's parents set up the Amy Winehouse Foundation. It would have been Amy's twenty-eighth birthday. The foundation was created specifically to support young people struggling with alcohol and drug misuse, particularly those who are unable to pay for their own treatment. They can't go back and save Amy, but perhaps they can help to save others like her.

* * * * *

It's charming and upsetting to read old interviews and hear Amy talk about the future. The poster girl for heartbreak was ready to move on. She'd spent years looking at life through blues-tinted glasses, saying to *GQ* in 2007, 'Every bad situation is a blues song waiting to happen but I'm romantic. I fall in love every day. Not with people but with situations. The other day, I saw a tramp polishing his shoes. That just gripped my heart.' Later, she wanted to be happy. She craved it. She was ready to start writing 'winsome, pining songs' and dole out the love she'd been wasting on Blake to others who deserved it more, maybe even herself. She craved beauty. 'I don't want to do another record of "screw you" songs. It will be a romantic record. I am a very romantic person. I don't mean romantic in a flowers and chocolates kind of way. It's more like if it's raining, I'll go up to the window and press my nose against the glass and sigh at how beautiful it all looks.'

* * * * *

Amy Winehouse always seemed to exist both in and out of time. She was an icon of a specific moment in British culture, but her voice and her soul seemed to belong to another era. The dirty glamour of her downfall, once romanticized, has become a parable, a warning tale.

The cultural phenomenon of the '27 Club' is something people talk a lot about when it comes to Amy Winehouse. This is a group of hyper-visible, very talented creative people who all happen to have died at the age of 27. Brian Jones, Jimi Hendrix, Janis Joplin and Jim Morrison all died at that age, and all within a mere two-year span. When Kurt Cobain died at the feted age in 1994, the notion of the Club began. It became the subject of much discussion in the weeks following Amy's death, too. It's an age that's taken on mythic status, to the point where even I was secretly very slightly disappointed when the clock struck midnight on my twenty-eighth birthday. But really, this glamourized fallacy of mental illness, addiction and suffering going hand in hand with creativity is one that should be seen for what it is: a waste.

* * * * *

Q. Where do you see yourself in 10 years?

Amy: 'Well, I'll have at least three beautiful kids. I want to do at least four or five albums and I want to get them out of the way now. And then I want to take ten years out to go and have kids, definitely. I never used to be broody, but then I realized that I'm turning into a soppy bitch. Goodness in life comes from a sense of achievement and you'd get that from having a child and putting it before yourself.'

And just three months before her death:

'I'm not a natural born performer. I'm quite shy really? You know what it's like? I don't mean to be sentimental or soppy but it's a little bit like being in love, when you can't eat, you're restless, it's like that. But then the minute you go on stage, everything's OK. The minute you start singing.'

* * * * *

Further Reading

Books

Janis Winehouse, *Loving Amy: A Mother's Story* (Bantam Press, 2014)

Mitch Winehouse, *Amy, My Daughter* (HarperCollins, 2013)

Newspaper articles

'Amy Winehouse: the Q Interview', *The Independent*, 18 January 2004

'Charmed and Dangerous', *The Observer*, 1 February 2004

'Friends Reunited', *The Guardian*, 22 April 2007

'Bloodied and Bruised Amy Winehouse Stands by Husband Who "Saved her Life"', *The Daily Mail*, 24 August 2007

'"I Want You Back", Amy Winehouse's "Terrified" Mother Begs Her Daughter in Open Letter', *The Daily Mail*, 10 December 2007

'Amy Winehouse in Her Own Words', *The Guardian*, 22 July 2012

'Amy Winehouse: Why We Are All to Blame', *The Telegraph*, 2 July 2015

Websites

Amy Winehouse interview, pauldunoyer.com, 2004

'Amy and Blake: Love and Turmoil', BBC News, 21 July 2008

Documentaries

My Daughter Amy, Channel 4, 2010

Amy, dir. Asif Kapadia, 2015

Index

Index

Picture Credits

(numbered in order of appearance)

1. WENN Rights Ltd/Alamy

2. Rick Smee/Redferns/Getty Images

3. Screenshot from archival footage

4. FIG Fotos/Alamy

5. Photo by J. Quinton/WireImage/Getty Images

6. Matt Kent/Wireimage/Getty Images

7, 8. Photo by Dave M. Benett/Getty Images

9. Photo by JMEnternational/Redferns/Getty Images

10. Photo by Jon Furniss/WireImage/Getty Images

11. Photo by Mark Milan/FilmMagic/Getty Images

12. Mku/Shutterstock

13. Photo by JMEnternational/Redferns/Getty Images

14, 15. Photo by Peter Macdiarmid/Getty Images for NARAS

16. David Fisher/Shutterstock

17. Ben Stansall/AFP via Getty Images

18. Photo by Dave M. Benett/Getty Images

19. Edward Westmacott/Alamy